KEYS TO UNDERSTANDING ARTHRITIS

Elizabeth Vierck
Consultant in Gerontology

BARRON'S

DEDICATION: To the millions of seniors who live with the pain of arthritis

All inquiries should be addressed to:
Barron's Educational Series, Inc.
250 Wireless Boulevard
Hauppauge, New York 11788

Library of Congress Catalog Card No. 91-13179

International Standard Book No. 0-8120-4731-1

Library of Congress Cataloging-in-Publication Data

Vierck, Elizabeth, 1945-
    Keys to understanding arthritis / Elizabeth Vierck.
        p.   cm.—(Barron's retirement keys)
    ISBN 0-8120-4731-1
    1. Arthritis—Popular works.   I. Title.   II. Series.
RC933.V54   1991
616.7'22—dc20   91-13179
                                                         CIP

PRINTED IN THE UNITED STATES OF AMERICA
1234   5500   987654321

CONTENTS

ACKNOWLEDGMENTS

No nonfiction book is ever written by the author alone. It is impossible to list in this small space the names of all people who helped me pull together the information for this book. I am indebted to them all for their invaluable help.

I would particularly like to thank Dr. Lawrence E. Shulman, director of the National Institute of Arthritis and Musculoskeletal and Skin Diseases, Dr. Arthur I. Grayzel, senior vice president, medical affairs of the Arthritis Foundation, and Don L. Riggin, president and CEO of the foundation, for taking time out of their busy schedules to submit to extensive interviews. All three contributed a great deal to the book.

In addition, I am genuinely impressed by the spirit of cooperation of the Arthritis Foundation staff. Specifically, I would like to thank Roy Scott, of the foundation, who was instrumental in arranging interviews and supplying me with a wealth of information from foundation resources. Barbara Welden and the staff of the National Institute of Arthritis and Musculoskeletal and Skin Diseases were equally helpful.

And, as always, I am grateful to my husband, Craig Boyle, for his solid, sagacious, gentle way in the world and to my girls, Lina and Katie, for their enthusiastic companionship.

INTRODUCTION

It is a common assumption that arthritis is "just old age and nothing can be done about it." The purpose of this book is to dispel this myth and to provide indispensable information about how to treat the key arthritic conditions that affect older people. *Keys to Understanding Arthritis* also provides practical details on how to live with arthritis-related limitations. Important information throughout the book has been provided by Dr. Lawrence E. Shulman, director of the National Institute of Arthritis and Musculoskeletal and Skin Diseases, Dr. Arthur Grayzel, senior vice president, medical affairs of the Arthritis Foundation, and Don L. Riggin, President and CEO of the foundation. Their contributions are invaluable.

The first four keys in the book cover general information about arthritis and aging. Keys 6 through 20 cover the full range of conditions that are included under the arthritis "umbrella" as it affects seniors. These conditions include the slight twinges that come with a mild case of osteoarthritis; the life-changing, debilitating symptoms that far too often accompany rheumatoid arthritis; and the acute, sudden pain of gout. The names of some of the conditions described here may be unfamiliar. Polymyalgia rheumatica, for example, is a disease that causes severe weakness and stiffness in muscles and joints. It is included here because it mysteriously affects primarily older adults. Another condition that is discussed, Sjögren's syndrome, often accompanies other forms of arthritis and causes dry eyes and a dry mouth. The syndrome may affect many older adults who are not even aware that they have it.

Key 21 includes tips from Dr. Arthur Grayzel, senior vice president, medical affairs of the Arthritis Foundation, on how to prevent and lessen the course of noninflammatory types of arthritis. Key 22 is a guide to the health personnel you are likely to see over the course of treatment for arthritis. Keys 23 through 40 describe the most common treatments for arthritis, including medications and management of pain. Discussed in these keys are (1) getting the right kind of exercise to keep joints from becoming stiff and/or deformed, (2) relaxation techniques such as focusing and biofeedback, and (3) approaches to pain management such as the popular TENS (transcutaneous electrical nerve stimulation).

Finally, the last keys discuss ways to detect quack remedies, how to adjust to the limitations that can occur with the more severe forms of arthritis, the newest research discoveries relating to arthritis and its treatment, and finally, information on how to get help from programs such as those offered by the Arthritis Foundation.

It is my hope that the information in this book will help dispel the myth that nothing can be done about arthritis. In addition, if you or someone you love has arthritis, I hope that you will take advantage of the many excellent resources for treating and living with rheumatic conditions that are described here.

E.V.
Denver, Colorado

1

ARTHRITIS DEFINED

The culprit behind many of the aches and pains of old age is arthritis. As writer Isaac Asimov says, "What most people think of as aging is really arthritis." Arthritis has the dubious distinction of being the leading chronic condition causing limitation in older persons; the Arthritis Foundation estimates that 97 percent of all people over 60 have enough arthritis to show up on X-rays. Its distressing symptoms affect more people than any other condition, including heart disease. An estimated 37 million Americans of all ages have arthritis; 7 million have long-term disabilities resulting from it. Increasing life expectancy means that the number of arthritis victims is burgeoning.

While arthritis is prevalent in modern times, it is not a modern condition; it has been found in the skeletons of prehistoric man. It is also not exclusive to human beings but is common among most warm-blooded animals (although, strangely, it is found in mice, but not rats). It has even been found in dinosaur skeletons.

Arthritis literally means inflammation of the joint (the area where two bones meet). The inflammation may be caused by damage resulting from the normal "wear and tear" that takes place over decades of use, as well as by disease, injury, metabolic disorders, or infection. In response to the injury, tissues become inflamed. The inflammation, in turn, causes swelling, redness, pain, and loss of motion in the affected area as well as, in a painful vicious cycle, more damage and more inflammation. Over time, bones and other joint tissues become stiff, distorted, dislocated, and sometimes immobile.

Because we use at least one joint every time we move, arthritis affects every daily activity, from drinking a cup of coffee to lifting a child. It usually, but not always, lasts a lifetime. Happily, however, the symptoms of many forms of arthritis wax and wane, and many victims have periods of remission when they feel no symptoms.

How many types of arthritis are there? There are over 100 forms of arthritis, ranging from osteoarthritis, which is very common in older persons but usually blessedly mild, to rheumatoid arthritis, which is less prevalent but frequently painful and disabling.[1] While extremely painful, gout is the form that can be treated the most successfully. Generalized aching resulting from stress, fatigue, or depression is not arthritis but is often mistaken for it.

Dr. Lawrence E. Shulman, director of the National Institute on Arthritis, Musculoskeletal Diseases and Skin Disorders, emphasizes that researchers have made remarkable progress in understanding arthritis. However, there is still much more to learn. For example, research has shown that there may be genetic reasons why some people get osteoarthritis and others do not. According to Shulman, this finding and others demonstrate that many forces are at work that we don't yet understand.

Dr. Shulman points out that it is important to remember three things about arthritis. First, as we have noted, there is not one but many kinds of arthritis. Second, not everyone gets it. No type of arthritis, including osteoarthritis, occurs in everyone.

---

[1]For the sake of clarity in this book, we have used the broad definition of arthritis to include all the rheumatic conditions that commonly affect the musculoskeletal systems of older adults.

Third, Shulman says, "It is important for the person with arthritis to keep an open mind about what is going to happen." The outlook for a person with arthritis varies not only according to the particular form of the condition but also within each disorder. For example one person with osteoarthritis may experience slight twinges, while another may become disabled and even require surgery.

Types of arthritis prevalent during the later years: Some types of arthritis strike primarily older adults. They are osteoarthritis, pseudogout, osteoporosis, Paget's disease, polymyalgia rheumatica, and giant cell arteritis. Other forms of arthritis don't necessarily favor older adults but have characteristics that are different in old age. They include rheumatoid arthritis, systemic lupus erythematosus, Sjögren's syndrome, polymyositis, progressive systemic sclerosis, gout, and infectious arthritis.

It is important to learn about the numerous types of arthritis that can affect you in later life, because each condition can be helped and has its own course of treatment. If you have the symptoms of arthritis, you may be tempted to say, "Why should I see a doctor? It's just arthritis—there's nothing they can do." But there are in fact many things that can be done, from medication to joint protection, that can relieve symptoms and reduce long-term effects. First, however, the doctor must determine what type of arthritis you have before deciding how serious it is and how to treat it.

2

TYPES OF ARTHRITIS; SYMPTOMS AND TREATMENT

Types of arthritis: Arthritis in its numerous forms affects a range of body structures and has several causes, including:

- *inflammation of the thin tissue lining the joint* (the synovial membrane): This is characteristic of rheumatoid arthritis and other inflammatory joint disorders.
- *cartilage breakdown* (cartilage is gristle-like tissue covering the end of bones): This is the "wear and tear" phenomenon. It is universal in older adults.
- *metabolic disorders:* This is characteristic of the very painful form of arthritis called gout. Gout is caused by urate crystals which are deposited in the joint space causing inflammation.
- *arthritis caused by infection:* This is inflammation of the joint space caused by bacteria, viruses, fungi, and parasites.
- *arthritis caused by injury:* This is the result of excessive stress on specific joints. Ballerinas, for example, often suffer from arthritis in their feet, and tennis buffs may develop "tennis elbow."
- *arthritis of the spine:* Stiffness is a major characteristic of this condition, the most serious form of which is ankylosing spondylitis. In many cases, the spine becomes rigid.
- *arthritis caused by other conditions:* In this case damage to the joint results from such diseases as psoriasis,

4

hemophilia, sickle cell anemia, diabetes, endocrine disorders, or hepatitis.

Symptoms: The symptoms of arthritis range from mild aching to severe pain. Extreme forms can result in permanent disability and disfigurement. Other forms such as gout may be temporary. The Arthritis Foundation's Dr. Grayzel states that you should call a doctor when low-grade symptoms have persisted for at least three weeks. In other words, if you wake up with aches and pains one morning when it is about to snow and the pain disappears two days later when it is sunny, you do not need a doctor's attention for your symptoms. On the other hand, if symptoms persist, you should discuss them with a doctor to avoid permanent disability. Here are the type of symptoms you should watch out for:

- swelling in one or more joints.
- early morning stiffness.
- recurring pain or tenderness in any joint.
- inability to move a joint normally.
- obvious redness and warmth in a joint.
- unexplained weight loss, fever, or weakness combined with joint pain.[2]

Treatment: Many people think that nothing can be done about arthritis. However, *every* form can be treated. Treatment may include mild to moderate exercises, physical therapy, medication (usually aspirin or nonsteroidal anti-inflammatory drugs), improving nutrition, pain relief techniques such as applying heat and cold, rest, and splints. Surgery, with or without joint replacement, is the last resort for individuals with severe damage. Fortunately, for those who must go this route, surgery for arthritis has become increasingly successful and can bring welcome relief from pain.

---

[2]Recommended by the Arthritis Foundation.

Unfortunately, far too many arthritis sufferers develop disabilities because they delay getting medical care. According to a recent study by the Centers for Disease Control six million people, or 2.5 percent of the population, believe they have arthritis but have not consulted a doctor about it.[3]

[3]"Arthritis Without Medical Care," *Arthritis Today*, July-August 1990, p. 14.

3

ABOUT JOINTS

Because arthritis is a group of diseases that mainly attacks the joints, it is helpful to know what joints are, how they work, and what happens when they are assaulted by an arthritis-related disorder.

A joint is the juncture where two bones meet. Joints give us our mobility and flexibility; without them we would walk and talk like robots. Every movement of the body involves a joint that provides strength, support, movement, or all three. Unfortunately, joints are highly susceptible to injury because they are used so frequently and because they are held together by relatively fragile ligaments.

Types of joints: There are three types of joints—the synarthrodial, amphiarthrodial, and diarthrodial. *Synarthrodial* joints are immobile and do not develop inflammation. Examples are joints in the skull. *Amphiarthrodial* joints, such as those in the vertebrae, move only slightly. *Diarthrodial* joints are freely movable and include joints of the knee or hip. Both amphiarthrodial and diarthrodial joints can develop inflammation.

The parts of a joint: The bones in a joint are protected from grinding against each other in a number of ways. The ends of the bones are covered by a shock absorber called *cartilage,* a tough, elastic tissue that prevents direct contact between bones (Figure 3-1). According to rheumatologist Dr. Lawrence Shulman, recent research has shown that, counter to previous assumptions, cartilage is a very lively part of the body where a lot of changes take place.

7

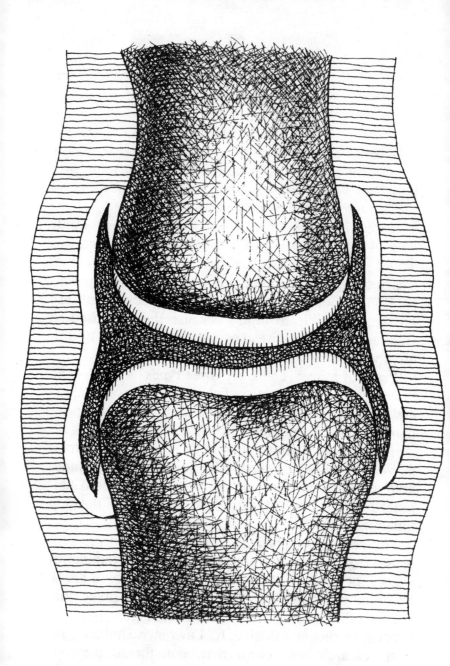

Figure 3–1: Illustration courtesy of The Arthritis Foundation, *The Arthritis Fact Book for the Media*.

All joints are covered by a capsule that contains an inner lining called a synovial membrane. The membrane releases drops of a substance called joint fluid (synovial fluid) into the space between the bones to nourish the cartilage and keep the joints lubricated.

Muscles, tendons, and ligaments provide support to joints and help bones to move in the right direction. Muscles and tendons move the bones. *Muscles* are elastic tissues that contract to enable the body to move, and *tendons* are bands of fibrous tissue that connect muscles to bones. *Ligaments* are like tendons except they connect bones to each other. In addition, *bursae* (soft, fluid-filled sacs that separate the muscles from bones and other muscles) help to maintain smooth muscle movement.

Although most forms of arthritis affect the parts of the body mentioned here, some forms can also harm other parts of the body, such as the blood vessels or skin.

Inflammation: Most forms of arthritis include inflammation in joints (Figure 3-2). Inflammation is the way that tissues react to injury. It is characterized by pain, swelling, heat, and redness.

In rheumatoid arthritis a mass called pannus forms in the joint from the inflammation of the synovial membrane. Once inflammation occurs, the body's immune system comes to the defense of the area and attacks the cause of the problem. Normally, once the immune system has done its job, the area heals and becomes healthy again, and the inflammation leaves. Arthritis occurs when the inflammation does not leave but sets up a vicious cycle of more inflammation. In some disorders, called autoimmune diseases, the immune system goes awry and attacks healthy parts of the body.

Joints and aging: According to Dr. Arthur Grayzel, medical director of the Arthritis Foundation, as joints

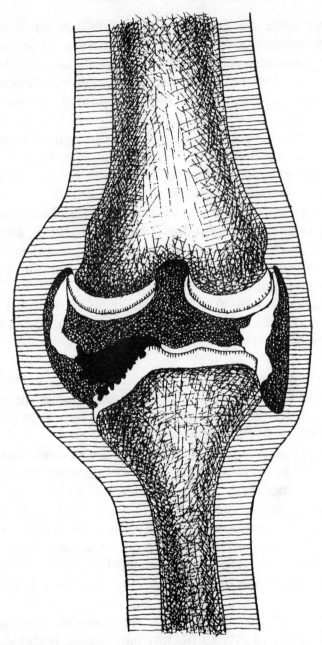

Figure 3–2: Illustration courtesy of The Arthritis Foundation, *The Arthritis Fact Book for the Media.*

age, muscles and ligaments lose their elasticity, leading to a reduced range of motion. (His suggestions for countering this loss are discussed in Key 21). In addition, all older persons experience changes in their cartilage as a result of the physical stress of decades of activity. Grayzel emphasizes that this type of change is *not* due to osteoarthritis, as often assumed; true osteoarthritis includes severe cartilage damage, significant pain, and loss of mobility, commonly starting in the fifth and sixth decades of life.

According to Dr. Grayzel, everyone experiences joint pain with aging. The key to age-related pain is that it comes and goes and is not continual, whereas in osteoarthritis the symptoms are persistent. Age-related pain may be due to muscle problems, inelasticity of ligaments, or cumulative injury, says Dr. Grayzel. In addition, falling is more common in the later years, and recovery is slow, which can cause pain in the joints. Some pain in the joints is also related to weather. Finally, Grayzel points out that it is hard to get a complete picture of what causes aches and pains at older ages, because it is difficult for researchers to get access to the necessary tissue to study it.

4

OSTEOARTHRITIS

What is osteoarthritis? Osteoarthritis[4] has been around so long it's a good bet that Adam and Eve felt its aches and pains as they grew older. It is one of the oldest and most common diseases of mankind, as well as the most frequently occurring type of arthritis. In fact, according to Dr. Shulman, half of all forms of arthritis may be related in some way to osteoarthritis.

Dr. Grayzel describes osteoarthritis as a condition in which cartilage is lost and damaged and in which changes in the underlying bone occur. These characteristics are distinctive and can be seen on an X-ray or in a piece of cartilage examined under a microscope. Osteoarthritis also involves soreness and loss of joint mobility. In addition, the muscles serving the joint become weak, sometimes affecting body movement and coordination.

Three myths about osteoarthritis. There are three common myths about osteoarthritis, according to Dr. Shulman. They are:

- Everyone who lives long enough will get osteoarthritis.
- Osteoarthritis is a natural consequence of the aging process.
- Osteoarthritis results from wear and tear on the joints.

---

[4]Physicians use a baffling array of names for the type of arthritis described in this chapter, including osteoarthritis, osteoarthrosis, arthrosis, degenerative joint disease, degenerative arthritis, and hypertrophic arthritis. For the sake of consistency, the author has chosen to use the term *osteoarthritis,* which is preferred by the Arthritis Foundation, throughout this book.

All three of these common assumptions are wrong. For example, a host of recent studies has shown that wear and tear is not the cause of osteoarthritis. Further, people sometimes experience pain in the joints that is erroneously labeled osteoarthritis. This type of pain is sometimes called soft tissue rheumatism or fibrositis (Key 12).

Where does osteoarthritis strike? Osteoarthritis can assault any joint but usually occurs in the knees, hands, hips, feet, and spine. It may also affect some finger joints, the joints at the base of the thumb, the joint at the base of the big toe, or any joint that has been injured. It rarely touches the wrists, elbows, shoulders, ankles, or jaw, except as a result of injury or unusual stress. A recent survey of people with osteoarthritis found that 75 percent had it in their knees, 60 percent in their hands, about 33 percent in the spine, 25 percent in their hips, and a small percent in their ankles and shoulders.

Osteoarthritis is chronic. In other words, there is no cure for it; once it develops, it remains an unwelcome companion for life.

Who develops osteoarthritis? Until recently, researchers assumed that virtually every person over age 60 has osteoarthritis. However, according to Dr. Grayzel, it has been shown that aging and osteoarthritis do not necessarily go hand in hand. While the disease is common in later years, this is not the result of changes taking place as part of the aging process but because the conditions for osteoarthritis take decades to develop.

Some people develop osteoarthritis early in life. They appear to have a form of the condition that differs from the type contracted later in life. For some individuals, osteoarthritis progresses very slowly, while for others symptoms come on rapidly. According to Dr.Grayzel, research is just beginning to answer some of the questions about who gets the disease and why it can take such different courses in different people.

Osteoarthritis strikes more women than men and is related to heredity, poor posture, and injury to the joints. In addition, the heavier an individual is, the more likely it is that osteoarthritis will develop in the joints that must carry the extra weight. Weight loss can significantly relieve symptoms.

What causes osteoarthritis? There are two major types of osteoarthritis, differentiated by cause. **Primary osteoarthritis** has no clear origin, but recent research suggests that certain forms run in families. **Secondary osteoarthritis** is caused by an identifiable problem such as old fractures, infections, damage from other diseases (such as gout), calcium deposits, and overuse of drugs.

Is there a cure for osteoarthritis? Older persons with osteoarthritis can and do enjoy an active life. Though there is no cure for the disease, it can be controlled and pain and discomfort can be minimized. Happily, it does not cripple or disfigure as rheumatoid arthritis often does, and it does not affect the entire body or cause an accompanying feeling of sickness.

Symptoms: Many people whose osteoarthritis shows up on X-rays never experience any symptoms of the disease. Those who do are likely first to notice painful and mildly stiff joints after overuse, after a period of rest (early in the morning, for example), and sometimes in wet and cold weather. Osteoarthritis can affect coordination and posture. Each joint is affected differently, and each can be treated surgically with varying degrees of success.

The symptoms of osteoarthritis are limited to the joints and, in most cases, are not severe. However, according to Dr. Grayzel, the symptoms of true osteoarthritis are persistent and do not wax and wane.

The hips. Pain from osteoarthritis may be felt around the groin or inner thigh. Referred pain (pain felt far away from the affected joint) may also be felt in the buttocks, knee, or on the side of the thigh. The pain may cause a limp. If the disease becomes severe, the hip joint may need to be replaced with an artificial one. Hip joint replacement has been performed successfully on older persons.

The knees. Tenderness and pain in the knees may be felt with movement. The victim may feel "grating" or "catching" in the joint and often find it painful to climb stairs. In advanced cases, a surgeon can use an instrument called an arthroscope to remove some of the loose fragments within the joint or can replace it with an artificial one. However, the latter is generally less successful than hip surgery.

The hands. Pain is felt in the small joints of the hands. Hands are one of the most common sites for osteoarthritis. Bony growths (spurs) form in the joints. (Spurs are hard nodules and differ from the soft, spongy swelling found in rheumatoid arthritis.) Spurs in the end of the fingers, called Heberden's nodes, are most common. Those in the middle are called Bouchard's nodes. Heberden's nodes strike most often in women and tend to run in families. Both types of nodes may appear in one finger and then spread to others.

When osteoarthritis is present in the hands, the base of the thumb is almost always affected. Other symptoms of the disease are redness, swelling, tenderness, and aching in the joints, as well as tingling and/or numbness in the fingertips. In severe cases, the fingers may overlap in a condition sometimes referred to as "pick-up-sticks." Although osteoarthritis of the hands can be painful and unattractive, functioning is usually not affected. Orthopedic surgery can be successfully performed on the hands.

The feet. When osteoarthritis affects the feet, pain and tenderness are felt in the large joint at the bottom of the big toe. Tight shoes and high heels worsen the pain. There is very little a surgeon can do to ease this form of osteoarthritis except for fusing the joint.

The spine. Pain from osteoarthritis in the spine may be felt in the base of the head, neck, legs, lower back (*sciatica*), or down the arms. Sufferers may experience stiffness in the lower back or neck, as well as weakness or numbness in the arms or legs. Spinal osteoarthritis can be extremely painful and limiting because it puts direct pressure on nerves. Surgery for osteoarthritis of the spine is, unfortunately, not very successful.

Diagnosis: Physicians can often diagnose osteoarthritis on the basis of a physical examination and medical history. Diagnosis may also require X-rays to see if the changes in joints and bones that usually accompany the disease are present, joint aspiration (in which fluid is drained from the joint and examined), and blood tests to determine if other diseases are present.

Treatment: People experiencing symptoms should see a doctor who will set up a treatment program to minimize progression of the disease. Treatment will consist of a combination of the following: joint protection (Key 38), exercise (Keys 21 and 32), medication (Keys 24 to 31), hot and cold treatments (Key 34), weight control (Key 33), and surgery, if necessary (Key 40).

5

RHEUMATOID ARTHRITIS

What is rheumatoid arthritis, and where does it strike? Rheumatoid arthritis is the second most common form of arthritis. It is an autoimmune disease in which the immune system goes awry and, instead of protecting the body against disease, turns against it, especially the joints. Rheumatologist Dr. Lawrence Shulman estimates that about half of all people with rheumatoid arthritis become disabled by it.

In rheumatoid arthritis, the synovial membrane (the inner lining of the capsule surrounding all joints) becomes inflamed, causing it to become thickened and to release more fluid than normal. The inflammation also causes the release of enzymes which causes the cartilage and bones to deteriorate. In particular, the enzymes destroy the articular cartilage, which acts as a cushion between joint bones. In addition, fluid accumulates in the joint. Eventually the bones in the joint touch each other and the inflammation and accompanying pain disappear. However, so does the ability of the joint to function. At this point the joints become fused.

Who develops rheumatoid arthritis? Rheumatoid arthritis affects over seven million people, or one of every 100 Americans. Roughly two out of every 100 persons have a mild form of the disease. Rheumatoid arthritis tends to hit between the ages of 20 and 50, although it may occur later. The disease is more common for women than men; three of four rheumatoid arthritis victims are women.

17

What causes rheumatoid arthritis? The cause of rheumatoid arthritis is not yet known. However, some theories suggest that a bacterium or virus may trigger the disease in those people with a tendency toward it.

Is there a cure for rheumatoid arthritis? At present there is no cure. However, education about the disease and treatment are very important factors in minimizing its effects and slowing its progress.

Rheumatoid factor: Eighty percent of adults with rheumatoid arthritis have an antibody called rheumatoid factor present in their blood streams and joints. Rheumatoid factor interacts with the individual's normal gamma globulin to cause inflammation. It is important to note that presence of the rheumatoid factor does *not* necessarily mean that you will develop the disease; about one in five of all people over age 60 have positive rheumatoid factor, but only a minority have the disease. Moreover, it is possible for people who do *not* have the factor to contract rheumatoid arthritis.

Anemia: An abnormally low number of red blood cells (anemia) often occurs along with rheumatoid arthritis and can cause extreme fatigue. This form of anemia is unfortunately *not* helped by iron or vitamins. An iron deficiency anemia can also result from taking anti-inflammatory drugs to treat the disease.

Symptoms: Many victims of rheumatoid arthritis experience mild symptoms that often come and go. Blessedly, this on-again, off-again course means periods free of pain and inflammation. However, as the disease progresses, the symptoms flare up more often, with shorter and shorter periods of relief.

Approximately one fourth of the older adults who develop rheumatoid arthritis have a very acute initial episode. The following are the most common symptoms of rheumatoid arthritis:

- inflammation.
- sudden onset.
- redness, warmth, pain, swelling, and stiffness in several joints on symmetrical sides of the body. In other words, if the elbow joint on the left side is affected, the right elbow will also be affected.
- soft, spongy swelling in the joints.
- fatigue, soreness, stiffness, and aching, commonly occurring in the morning and after sitting or lying still.
- a feeling of being sick, loss of appetite, weight loss, and fever. Other possible body changes include anemia, inflamed eyes, pleurisy, and lumps or nodules at the back of the elbows that come and go.

The joints most often affected by rheumatoid arthritis are the hands, elbows, hips, and knees. The disease does not affect only joints; it is a systemic disease, touching the whole body. Its victims are sick—they feel weak and listless and may lack appetite and lose weight. The inflammation also may advance to other parts of the body, including organs and muscles.

Victims of rheumatoid arthritis may also have the dry eyes and mouth of Sjögren's syndrome, which is described in Key 17.

Diagnosis: Rheumatoid arthritis is diagnosed through a medical history, physical examination, and laboratory tests. The latter confirm the presence of inflammation in the system. The following tests are often performed:
- blood test for rheumatoid factor (see above).
- blood test for sedimentation rate, which measures how fast red blood cells settle to the bottom of a tube. People with chronic inflammation of any kind, including that found in rheumatoid arthritis, have cells that fall faster than normal.

19

- blood test for anemia.
- joint aspiration, in which fluid is drained from swollen joints to determine if the condition is caused by another problem, such as infection.
- biopsy in which small bits of tissue are removed and examined.
- X-rays to detect the amount of damage in specific joints.

Treatment: Treatment of rheumatoid arthritis depends on the individual and the severity of the condition. Dr. Shulman emphasizes that "becoming educated about rheumatoid arthritis is important and helpful in its treatment—maybe even as important as taking medications." Treatment may include taking the following types of drugs: nonsteroidal anti-inflammatory drugs (Key 26); high doses of aspirin (Key 24); corticosteroids (Key 29); drugs that aid remission, such as gold salts and penicillamine (Key 27); drugs that suppress the immune system (Key 28); and antimalarials (Key 31).

One approach to treating rheumatoid arthritis that is gaining popularity is to give one or several of the stronger medications early in the disease process before too much damage has been done to the joints. In the past these drugs were usually prescribed only after a series of simpler drugs had been tried first. In addition, rest, exercise, heat treatments, joint protection, managing stress and depression, and physical and rehabilitation therapy may be beneficial. Surgery is a last resort but can be effective.

6

OSTEOARTHRITIS AND RHEUMATOID ARTHRITIS: HOW TO TELL THE DIFFERENCE

Osteoarthritis and rheumatoid arthritis are often confused. A general rule of thumb is that the effects of osteoarthritis are often kinder and more gentle than those of rheumatoid arthritis. Inflammation does not usually accompany osteoarthritis, and the disease is not systemic, meaning that it does not affect the whole body. The opposite is true for rheumatoid arthritis.

In short, if you have a feeling of pain and stiffness in specific joints after rest or overuse but you do *not* have a swelling in the affected areas accompanied by a feeling of sickness, your symptoms are probably caused by osteoarthritis and not by rheumatoid arthritis.

Exhibit 6-1 presents some of the differences between osteoarthritis and rheumatoid arthritis.

Exhibit 6-1.

Osteoarthritis	Rheumatoid Arthritis
• Develops slowly	• Often develops suddenly
• Usually doesn't cause redness, warmth, or swelling	• Causes redness, warmth, and swelling
• Affects only certain joints	• Affects many joints
• Often affects only one side of the body at first	• Usually affects joints on both sides of the body

- Marked by bony growth
- Doesn't affect the whole body
- Doesn't cause general feeling of sickness

- Marked by soft, spongy swelling
- Affects the whole body
- Causes a general feeling of sickness

7

SYSTEMIC LUPUS ERYTHEMATOSUS

What is lupus? Systemic lupus erythematosus, also called SLE or, more commonly, lupus, is a potentially serious form of arthritis that can involve vital organs. Fortunately, however, for many, the disease is mild. Lupus has been around at least since Hippocrates described it in 400 B.C.

Lupus has been called the "great impersonator" because its symptoms are frequently diagnosed as resulting from another disease. For example, a victim may see a physician for a kidney problem which turns out to be caused by lupus. About one in five individuals with SLE develops the disease after the age of 50. The later in life the disease develops, the less severe it is likely to be.

Lupus may be brought on by drugs and the incidence of drug-induced lupus increases with age. At present about 50 drugs are known to cause lupus symptoms.

Just two decades ago a diagnosis of lupus was a death warrant. Now, however, it can be controlled with steroids, although the long-term use of these drugs creates its own problems.

Where does lupus strike? A unique feature of lupus is a characteristic rash that spreads across the nose and cheeks. Ninety percent of patients also have joint pain, but, fortunately, arthritic deformities are rare. Lupus also affects the muscles, skin, kidneys, the nervous system, lungs, heart, and blood-forming organs. Like rheumatoid arthritis, the disease waxes and wanes, and there may be periods of almost complete remission.

Like rheumatoid arthritis, lupus is an autoimmune disorder, meaning that the body's immune system attacks the body itself. In lupus, the body's production of antibodies, which normally helps to defend against disease, goes off kilter, and the antibodies actually work against the body's own tissues even without the threat of disease from bacteria, which is usually the factor that arouses immune system activity.

People with lupus sometimes develop other problems, including the following:

- If the kidneys fail, waste products build up in the blood, and the victim must use dialysis to cleanse the blood. Kidney transplants are a last resort.
- Normal natural defenses against infection are affected, particularly for those taking corticosteroids and immunosuppressive drugs.
- Lupus victims may test positively for syphilis. However, *there is no relationship between the two*.

Who develops lupus? Lupus was formerly thought to be rare. However, current statistics suggest that in the United States 16,000 people have the condition. Like rheumatoid arthritis, lupus is predominantly a woman's disease; for every man who gets lupus, eight to ten women are stricken. Every one in 1000 to 2000 people— but one in 700 women—have lupus. Some estimates suggest that lupus is more common than muscular dystrophy, multiple sclerosis, or leukemia. Most victims contract it while they are young adults, but the disease does not discriminate against age—older adults may develop it, or dormant symptoms may appear in later life. Lupus hits blacks and some Asian and North American groups more often than whites; in fact, one in 250 black women develops lupus.

What causes lupus? The cause of lupus is not known. However, a small study by Dr. Marc Hochberg at Johns Hopkins University done in conjunction with the

United States Centers for Disease Control identified one possible risk factor for lupus—the use of hair dye. However, Dr. Hochberg warns that further study is needed to confirm these results.[5]

Is there a cure for lupus? There is no cure, but the disease can be helped by steroids.

Three types of lupus: There are three forms of the disease—discoid, systemic, and subacute cutaneous lupus. *Discoid* lupus is a chronic disease of the skin. Victims of systemic lupus may have discoid lupus, although the reverse does not apply; discoid lupus rarely progresses to systemic lupus. *Systemic* lupus, like all systemic diseases, involves the entire body. *Subacute cutaneous* lupus, which has recently been identified, includes skin lesions similar to (but more widespread than) those in discoid lupus and a mild systemic lupus. Kidney disease does not occur in this form of lupus. This Key covers systemic lupus only.

Symptoms: Pain in the joints, caused by inflammation of the synovial membrane, is the primary symptom of lupus. Other symptoms depend on which organs the disease attacks. In general, however, the following symptoms are characteristic of the disease:
• low grade fever, weakness, fatigue, and weight loss.
• skin rash on the face, neck, and arms (called a butterfly rash when it involves the nose and cheeks). The rash may get worse when exposed to ultraviolet light.
• painful, red, warm, swollen joints.
• extreme sensitivity to sun (photosensitivity).
• a feeling of stiffness in the morning on waking.
• muscle aches, swollen glands, lack of appetite, easy bruising, hair loss, and nausea and vomiting.
• anemia.

---

[5]Joseph Wallace, "Can Arthritis Be Prevented?" *Arthritis Today*, July-August 1990, p. 48.

- increased vulnerability to infections or bleeding.
- increased tendency to form blood clots.
- pain on breathing or shortness of breath.
- kidney problems.
- edema (swelling) of the legs.
- Raynaud's phenomenon, in which the feet and hands turn blue on exposure to cold.

Of these, the most common are mild joint pain especially in the morning, rashes, and chronic fatigue. Photosensitivity occurs in fewer than 40 percent of lupus victims.

Victims of lupus erythematosus may also have the dry eyes and mouth of Sjögren's syndrome (Key 17).

Diagnosis: Physicians perform a number of tests to check for lupus or to determine the degree of involvement of body organs.

- A blood test to verify the presence of a specific antibody called antinuclear antibody (or ANA), which is found in the blood of most lupus victims.
- Other blood tests, including some to determine the amount of damage to organs.
- Urinalysis to evaluate kidney function.
- A biopsy (if kidney damage is detected).
- Chest X-rays to evaluate potential chest and heart damage.
- Electrocardiograms and echocardiograms to check for heart involvement.

Strangely, some people with lupus have normal tests.

Treatment: Treatment for lupus varies according to which organs are involved and the extent of damage. However, general treatment includes: taking medications (Keys 24 to 29), rest during periods when the disease is active (Key 35), eating a balanced diet (Key 33), and staying out of the sun. Some lupus victims must follow low-salt diets to prevent edema or limited protein diets if kidney function is affected.

8

GOUT

What is gout and where does it strike? If you have sudden excruciating pain in the large joint of your big toe, you may have gout. Gout is a common and painful form of arthritis that also has the distinction of being the most responsive to treatment. The inherited condition is caused by a buildup of uric acid in the body.

Who develops gout? As rheumatoid arthritis and lupus are primarily women's diseases, gout is primarily a man's disease at younger ages. Women are generally protected from gout until menopause, at which point their incidence rises to match that of men of the same age. Many great men in history, from Michelangelo to Ben Franklin, have had the disease. Gout currently affects about one million Americans.

Many people express surprise that gout is a form of arthritis. The common assumption is that it is a disease of excess, afflicting paunchy men who eat and drink too much. This is not the case. However, gout sufferers do have to stay away from certain foods and alcohol.

What causes gout? Uric acid, a waste product, normally circulates in the blood until it passes through the kidneys. In gout, either the body produces too much uric acid or the kidneys become ineffective at removing it, or both. Attacks of gout occur when the uric acid crystals settle in the joints, inflaming the joint lining. The inflammation, in turn, irritates the nerve endings in the joint, causing extreme pain. In addition, cells rush to the afflicted joint in an attempt to correct the situation, creating even more obstruction. Uric acid crystals can also collect in the kidneys, leading to kidney failure. Gout is sometimes caused by specific drugs, such as diuretics and aspirin, that impede the kidneys' ability to eliminate uric acid. Other conditions, such as some types of cancer and diseases of the blood-forming organs, can also lead to an excess of uric acid (*hyperuricemia*) and gout. Sometimes uric acid crystals can also accumulate in cartilage and in growths that grow under the skin.

According to the Arthritis Foundation, an attack of gout can be brought on by:
- drinking too much alcohol.
- eating too many purine-rich foods. (Purine is a chemical found in certain foods that forms uric acid in the body.)
- surgery.
- a sudden, severe illness.
- crash diets.
- injury to the joint.

Is there a cure for gout? Attacks of gout subside after a few days. There may be no recurrence, or it may be years before another attack occurs. Some victims, however, may require treatment for the remainder of their life.

Symptoms: Gout can assault any joint, but it tends to prefer small joints and commonly inflames the large joint of the big toe. In older adults, it commonly strikes more than one joint. Although the pain will probably come on all of a sudden, uric acid may have been collecting in the blood for a long time. The first attack of gout commonly occurs at night. The joint is usually red or purple, shiny, and dry. It is also extremely tender; even the touch of bed covers causes excruciating pain. Fortunately, there are no symptoms between attacks. If gout attacks return, there will be increasingly shorter intervals between them and they will take longer to recede. While further attacks may include more joints, gout does not spread from joint to joint. Having an attack in one joint does not mean that you will have it in others. If the disease is not treated, deformity can occur.

After gout has been present for several years, deposits of uric acid called tophi can build up in the joints and surrounding tissues. Tophi look like lumps under the skin and, if not treated, can cause a fair amount of damage.

Diagnosis and treatment: The majority of gout victims have a condition called hyperuricemia, or excess uric acid in the blood. Colchicine™, the most specific drug for eliminating a gouty attack, has been around since the time of Hippocrates. Colchicine™ is so specific to gout it is used for diagnosis—if the condition responds to the drug, it is gout; if it doesn't, it isn't.

To determine if a patient has gout, doctors also take tests to measure the amount of uric acid in the blood and check for other types of arthritis, such as pseudogout, which resembles gout but is caused by calcium pyrophosphate dihydrate (CPPD) crystals instead of excess uric acid. The doctor also may remove fluid from the joint and examine it for crystals.

After an acute attack of gout has occurred, the physician will usually look for underlying causes for excess uric acid in the blood. Chronic gout is usually treated with daily doses of Colchicine™, unless side effects such as nausea and diarrhea develop (Key 30). Colchicine™ relieves current attacks and can prevent future attacks. It is usually taken orally. Colchicine™ can cause diarrhea, nausea, and abdominal cramps. To avoid such problems, the drug can be given via injection once every 24 hours. In addition, victims may have to take drugs to reduce levels of uric acid (Key 30).

Many gout victims want to take nonsteroidal anti-inflammatory drugs or corticosteroid medications to relieve the pain and inflammation of an acute attack. For information on these medications, see Keys 26 and 29. Gout victims should never treat their pain with aspirin because it inhibits the excretion of uric acid. Most individuals with gout keep the weight of sheets and other covers off the gouty area to prevent pain.

If you have gout, you may need to eliminate from your diet foods rich in a chemical called purine. Purine is a waste product that forms uric acid when it is broken down by the body. Purine-rich foods include organ meats such as liver and kidneys, sardines, anchovies, and legumes. You may also need to restrict your intake of alcohol because alcohol inhibits the excretion of uric acid. However, you should drink a lot of nonalcoholic fluids. Obese gout victims will be advised to lose weight.

Surgery for gout is done rarely and only if the victim has large tophi which are draining, infected, or interfering with the movement of joints.

9

PSEUDOGOUT

What is pseudogout? If you have sudden attacks of pain in one or more joints, you may have pseudogout. Pseudogout is a nonidentical twin to true gout. Pseudogout, like true gout, is caused by a build-up of crystals in joints, causing pain and inflammation, but the crystals are formed from calcium pyrophosphate dihydrate (CPPD), rather than from uric acid.

Pseudogout becomes more prevalent in older age. Most physicians check to see if patients with pseudogout have malfunctioning parathyroid glands, which are responsible for calcium metabolism, or hemochromatosis (iron overload).

Where does pseudogout strike? Pseudogout usually assaults larger joints, rather than the small joints of the toe or wrist. The knee is the most common site for pseudogout, but it may also affect the wrists, fingers, toes, hips, shoulders, elbows, and ankles.

Who develops pseudogout? While gout predominantly affects men and rheumatoid arthritis chiefly hits women, pseudogout strikes equal numbers of men and women. It is an older person's disease, occurring most often in people in their sixties. About six percent of people over age 70 have a mild form of the disease.

What causes pseudogout? The pain of pseudogout is caused by two effects of the CPPD crystals that build up the joints. First, the crystals weaken cartilage, causing it to break down and to provoke pain, stiffness, and a "grating" feeling in the joint. Second, the body reacts to the presence of the crystals with inflammation.

Pseudogout may result from injury or surgery. It can

31

also be caused by other diseases such as true gout, hemochromatosis (an excess of iron in the blood), hyperparathyroidism (an excess of calcium in the blood), and hypothyroidism (underactivity of the thyroid gland).

Is there a cure for pseudogout? Like gout, pseudogout is a chronic disease that runs in families and can not be cured, but it can be controlled with treatment.

Symptoms: The symptoms of pseudogout can resemble those of rheumatoid and osteoarthritis. Pseudogout may attack in one of two ways:

• sudden attacks of joint pain and swelling that eventually go away even if not treated.

• gradual stiffening, swelling, heat, and pain in any joints, lasting weeks or months. The pain worsens when the joint is moved.

Pseudogout victims may have one or both of these symptoms. Like many other forms of arthritis, the symptoms may flare up and subside, and there may be periods with no pain or other symptoms.

Diagnosis: To determine if a patient has pseudogout, doctors remove fluid from the joint and examine it for crystals. This procedure, called joint aspiration, is usually done in the doctor's office. Doctors may also take blood tests to rule out other kinds of arthritis and take X-rays of the joint cartilage to see if it has calcified. Calcification points specifically to pseudogout.

Treatment: As with any form of arthritis, treatment for pseudogout includes a combination of measures, depending on the complexity and severity of the problem. However, treatment may include joint aspiration; the use of nonsteroidal anti-inflammatory drugs (Key 26), corticosteroids (Key 29), or Colchicine™ (Key 30); rest (Key 35); exercise (Key 32); and joint protection (Key 38). A small number of people may require surgery (Key 40). At present there are no drugs that can prevent the buildup of crystals.

10

LYME DISEASE AND OTHER TYPES OF INFECTIOUS ARTHRITIS

What is infectious arthritis? If you have an infectious illness such as Lyme disease or mononucleosis and are now noticing pain in your joints, you may have infectious arthritis. Infectious or septic arthritis is joint inflammation that has been caused by a germ (bacterium, virus, or infection). The germ first causes an infection, such as Lyme disease, and then moves into the joints. Many types of germs may cause infectious arthritis. It usually hits the large joints, usually only one joint at a time.

Infectious arthritis is *not* contagious. However, infections such as gonorrhea that can be passed from one person to another can cause the condition.

Who develops infectious arthritis? Because of lower resistance, infected joints are seen more often in adults than in children or adolescents. In fact, if gonorrhea is excluded from the analysis, one in four cases of infectious arthritis occur in people over the age of 50. Older adults who have other conditions, such as malignancies, diabetes, and liver disease, may have more trouble fighting off the infections that can result in septic arthritis. In addition, some medications such as corticosteroids can reduce the ability to resist an infection.

What causes infectious arthritis? Most types are caused by a bacteria, but viruses and fungi can also lead to infectious arthritis.

The following infections can lead to infectious arthritis.

Lyme disease. Lyme disease is the newest kid on the arthritis block. It is caused by the bite of the Ixodes tick, which inserts a germ, called a spirochete, into the skin. The Ixodes tick, which is the size of a pinhead, is difficult to spot. It makes its home on deer and mice and can be found in woody areas during warm and hot months. Most cases of Lyme disease have been identified in New York, New Jersey, Rhode Island, Connecticut, Massachusetts, Wisconsin, and Minnesota.

Symptoms may take one to three weeks to develop. A characteristic ring-like rash develops around the tick bite; it is five to twenty inches in diameter, white in the center, and red on the outside. The center is hard and warm. The rash may also appear in other areas of the body.

Besides the rash, other symptoms of Lyme disease are flu-like symptoms; joint pain and swelling, particularly in the knees; sore throat, dry cough, stiff neck, and swollen glands; dizziness; and sensitivity to sunlight. The Arthritis Foundation recommends the following to prevent tick bites:

- wear long sleeves and pants.
- wear socks over pant legs.
- wear a hat.
- use tick repellent on clothes.
- shower after being in an area where ticks live and inspect your body thoroughly for ticks.

Gonococcal arthritis. This type of arthritis is caused by gonococcus, the sexually transmitted bacteria that causes gonorrhea. Gonococcal arthritis often affects the knee joints, tendons, and bursae. The disease can rapidly cause joint destruction, even before symptoms are felt and a diagnosis made. Gonorrhea can be treated with antibiotics.

Tuberculous arthritis. While now relatively rare, this type of arthritis was relatively common before the development of drugs to combat tuberculosis (TB). The condition can be cured with the long-term use of antibiotics.

Gram-positive bacteria. Gram-positive bacteria, when mixed with a laboratory solution called Gram's strain, take on a bluish-purple strain or color. Staphylococcus, streptococcus, and pneumococcus are all Gram-positive bacteria that can cause infectious arthritis. Staphylococcus, commonly referred to as a staph infection, is one of the most common causes of infectious arthritis. Individuals with rheumatoid arthritis, or who are taking steroids or immunosuppressive drugs to treat arthritis, are particularly susceptible to staph infections.

Viruses. Infectious arthritis can develop from a viral infection, such as infectious hepatitis, mumps, German measles, or mononucleosis. The condition usually, but not always, abates when the viral infections have subsided.

Fungi. Arthritis can develop very slowly from fungi found in soil, bird droppings, and some plants. Treatment requires treating the specific fungi.

Is there a cure for infectious arthritis? Fortunately, infectious arthritis is one of the few types of arthritis that is frequently completely curable.

If you have rheumatoid arthritis. Even if you have another form of arthritis, it is important to get checked for infectious arthritis if symptoms occur suddenly—particularly if only one joint is involved. It is easy for individuals with rheumatoid arthritis to mistake a bout of infectious arthritis for an attack of the original disease.

11

POLYMYALGIA RHEUMATICA (PMR) AND GIANT CELL ARTERITIS

What is polymyalgia rheumatica (PMR)? Polymyalgia rheumatica (PMR) is a disease that causes low-grade pain in the large central joints. For example, Dr. Arthur Grayzel of the Arthritis Foundation relates that patients with the condition point to their entire shoulder or hip rather than to specific tender spots when they describe their pain. Stiffness and muscle pain are also characteristic of the disease.

Dr. Grayzel also points out that polymyalgia rheumatica has symptoms that can be confused with fibromyalgia (Key 12). However, the former is treatable, while the latter,unfortunately, is not. In addition, polymyalgia rheumatica is more common in older adults, while fibromyalgia generally appears in women in their 30s and 40s.

Where does it strike? The parts of the body most often affected are the neck, shoulder, upper arms, lower back, hips, and/or thighs. PMR affects both sides of the body, and more than one area may be stricken.

Who develops PMR? The disease occurs primarily in older adults and rarely hits younger persons. The average age of onset is 65 to 70 years of age. It favors women by a ratio of two to one.

What causes PMR? The cause is not known. There is evidence that PMR runs in families.

Is there a cure for PMR? The normal course is for

the disease to disappear on its own after several years. However, proper treatment is vital.

Symptoms: Besides severe weakness and stiffness in muscles and joints, other symptoms of PMR include fatigue, night sweating, lack of appetite, a slight fever, and depression. Symptoms are usually most severe in the morning. Surprisingly, even though muscle symptoms are severe, the muscles appear normal on examination.

Diagnosis: There is no single test to detect PMR. However, blood tests show an elevated sedimentation rate, which indicates that inflammation is present. The doctor may order biopsies and tests to rule out other forms of arthritis and may perform muscle tests.

Treatment: People experiencing symptoms of PMR should see a doctor, who will set up a treatment program to minimize damage and alleviate symptoms. PMR responds to anti-inflammatory drugs (Key 26). Treatment may also include exercise (Keys 21 and 32), corticosteroids (Key 29), and rest (Key 35).

What is giant cell arteritis and where does it strike? PMR and giant cell arteritis overlap in many cases. According to the Arthritis Foundation, 10 to 15 percent of people with PMR have giant cell arteritis, and 40 percent of people with giant cell arteritis have PMR.

Giant cell arteritis is a narrowing of the arteries on the upper front sides of the head, the neck, and the arms, which can lead to blockage. It is potentially very damaging and can lead to violent headaches and blindness.

Who develops giant cell arteritis? While people with PMR may develop giant cell arteritis, it can also occur in people over 50 who do not have PMR.

Is there a cure? Like PMR, giant cell arteritis usually goes away after treatment.

Symptoms: The following are symptoms of giant cell arteritis:[6]
- Severe, persistent headaches
- Blurred or double vision or partial loss of vision
- Pain in jaw muscles when chewing or speaking
- Scalp tenderness
- Hearing loss
- Sore throat
- Cough
- Difficulty swallowing

Diagnosis: Giant cell arteritis victims have damaged temporal arteries. The doctor will determine if such damage is present by taking a sample of the artery and examining it.

Treatment: Giant cell arteritis is treated with corticosteroids (Key 29).

---

[6]Arthritis Foundation, A.F., Polymyalgia, *Rheumatica and Giant-Cell Arteritis*, 1990, p. 7.

12

FIBROMYALGIA

What is fibromyalgia? If you have pain in specific points on your body and disturbed sleep that is causing you to feel fatigued, you may have fibromyalgia. Fibromyalgia is not really an arthritic disease because it does not attack the joints. In the past it has been used as a catch-all diagnosis for unexplained pain. Specifically, however, the condition is chronic and painful. Like many of its arthritic cousins, its symptoms wax and wane. However, when the pain hits, it occurs in the ligaments, tendons, and muscles, not in the joints.

Because the syndrome affects the way that joints move, victims often think that their joints are involved. Fortunately, the condition does not cause deformity or crippling, and it usually lasts only three or four days. Fibromyalgia is also called fibrositis, muscular rheumatism, or fibromyalgia syndrome.

Fibromyalgia has baffled diagnosticians and researchers, and until recently there was a lot of disagreement over exactly what symptoms were involved. However, a committee of 24 researchers from arthritis centers around the United States has established criteria for diagnosing the condition. The standards specify that widespread pain as well as tenderness in 11 of 18 specific "trigger points" must be present to justify the diagnosis. However, according to Dr. Grayzel of the Arthritis Foundation, the most important symptom is a sleep disturbance. If his patients do not have this symptom, Dr. Grayzel looks elsewhere for a cause of the patient's problem.

Who develops fibromyalgia? While anyone can develop the condition, it commonly strikes women in their 30s and 40s. Dr. Grayzel points out that its symptoms can be confused with those of polymyalgia rheumatica, which is much more common among older adults (Key 12).

What causes fibromyalgia? The causes of fibromyalgia are not known. However, the Arthritis Foundation has delineated three major conditions associated with the disease. They are:

- physically unfit or poorly developed muscles. Fibrositis patients who exercise regularly improve the most.
- sleep disturbances. As mentioned above, people with fibrositis often have a sleep disorder in which the deepest or most restful stage of sleep is disturbed.
- stress, fatigue, and anxiety. While these may not cause the disease, they do make the condition worse.

Is there a cure for fibromyalgia? There is not a cure at this time, but in many cases the disease burns itself out.

Symptoms. Fibromyalgia is a little understood disease in which the symptoms are often vague. However, all victims experience the two major symptoms of pain and fatigue:

- pain or extreme tenderness in muscles at the point at which ligaments attach muscles to bone (the trigger points mentioned above). For a diagram of these points obtain a copy of *Fibromyalgia* (*Fibrositis*) from the closest chapter of the Arthritis Foundation or write: The Arthritis Foundation, P.O. Box 19000, Atlanta, GA 30326.
- fatigue or lack of muscle endurance resulting from a lack of restful sleep. Resting and/or napping during the day may help the problem. Many people who were thought to have "chronic fatigue syndrome" have been diagnosed with fibrositis.

Diagnosis: There are no lab tests or X-rays that can

be used to detect fibrositis, except to rule out other diseases. Physicians use medical histories and identification of "trigger points" to diagnose the disease.

Treatment: Doctors often concentrate on improving sleep as a major part of the treatment plan for fibrositis. They may prescribe an antidepressant to promote restful sleep. Paradoxically, sleeping pills may make the condition worse by disturbing the quality of sleep.

A second important part of treatment is getting regular low or nonimpact aerobic exercise. Steps may also be taken to control stress. Anti-inflammatory medications used for other forms of arthritis are generally *not* effective for fibrositis.

13

SCLERODERMA

What is scleroderma, and where does it strike?
Scleroderma is a relatively uncommon chronic disease
in which most victims have problems with their skin.
Scleroderma literally means "hard skin." The disease
can also affect joints, blood vessels, muscles, bones,and
internal organs.

There are two broad categories of scleroderma: localized and generalized. Localized scleroderma is the
less severe of the two. It affects primarily the skin,
although it can touch muscle and bone. Localized scleroderma does *not* lead to the more serious form of the
disease. Generalized scleroderma is systemic, meaning that it affects the whole body. It can attack the
skin, blood vessels, the digestive system, the heart,
lungs, kidneys, muscles, and joints. The severity of the
problems depends on the location and extent of the
disease.

Who develops scleroderma? Scleroderma strikes
most often in middle age, although older adults do contract it.

What causes scleroderma? While the cause is not
known, it is known that the bodies of scleroderma victims produce too much collagen, which is deposited in
the skin and affected parts of the body.

Is there a cure for scleroderma? At present there is
no cure, but drugs used in treatment are very effective.

Symptoms: The symptoms of scleroderma are different for everyone, and the various forms of scleroderma have unique symptoms. The following, adapted

from information provided by the Arthritis Foundation, is a short list of symptoms that may occur:
- skin changes such as hardening and thickening, especially on the hands, arms, and face; ulcers on fingers; decrease in hair over the affected area; change in skin color.
- swelling and puffiness of the hands and feet.
- hard, shiny fingers and toes.
- Raynaud's syndrome, a condition in which the feet and hands turn blue on exposure to cold.
- small reddish spots on fingers, palms, face, lips, and/or tongue.
- small white calcium lumps under the skin.
- painful and swollen joints.
- muscle weakness.
- general fatigue.
- dryness in tear ducts, salivary glands, and other areas of the body.
- digestive problems.
- heart and lung problems.
- kidney problems.

Victims of scleroderma may also have the dry eyes and mouth of Sjögren's syndrome. For information on Sjögren's, see Key 17.

Diagnosis: There is no single test to detect scleroderma. However, physicians commonly order a series of laboratory tests such as a biopsy and tests to check the immune system and lung functioning.

Treatment: Patients with scleroderma should see their doctor, who will set up a treatment program to minimize damage and alleviate symptoms. Treatment will consist of a combination of the following: joint protection (Key 38), exercise (Keys 21 and 32), medication (Keys 24 to 31), skin protection, and stress management (Key 35). In addition, scleroderma victims are advised to avoid exposure to the sun. The following recommendations are adapted from the Arthritis Foundation:

- Keep warm during cold weather. Those with Raynaud's phenomenon should always wear gloves when outdoors in cold weather or when in cold rooms.
- Use a cold room humidifier to keep skin moist.
- Avoid using strong detergents.
- Use bath products designed to prevent dry skin.

14

MYOSITIS (POLYMYOSITIS AND DERMATOMYOSITIS)

What is myositis? If you have muscle weakness in the hip and shoulder, you may have myositis. Myositis is a chronic disease that damages connective tissue and causes weakness. Connective tissue is fibrous tissue that holds together the cells of muscles, skin, cartilage, tendons, ligaments, blood vessels, bones, and some internal organs.

What are polymyositis and dermatomyositis? These two diseases are forms of myositis. Polymyositis is characterized by damage to the connective tissue of muscles, causing weakness and inflammation. Dermatomyositis is similar and includes a characteristic purplish skin rash. Both have symptoms that are also found in lupus, rheumatoid arthritis, and progressive systemic sclerosis. Older individuals with dermatomyositis may develop a malignancy.

Who develops polymyositis and dermatomyositis? Fortunately, neither disease is very common. They both tend to occur during the older years. In adults, myositis commonly hits between the ages of 30 and 60, and women are twice as likely to get it as men. In addition, persons past the age of 50 who have dermatomyositis may develop related tumors.

What causes polymyositis and dermatomyositis? The cause is unknown, but there is speculation that a defective immune system, a virus, or a combination of the two are involved.

Is there a cure for myositis? Myositis is a chronic disease and there is no known cure.

Symptoms: The major symptom is muscle weakness in the hips and shoulder area. Myositis may also affect muscles in the front of the neck, in the throat, and chest. Polymyositis victims may also develop a purplish skin rash on the face, knuckles, elbows, knees, and ankles. They also may develop Raynaud's syndrome, a condition in which the feet and hands turn blue on exposure to the cold (Key 18). Individuals with both kinds of myositis may also have an associated fever; weight loss; and painful, tender muscles and joints. Like many other rheumatic diseases, the symptoms of myositis often wax and wane.

Victims of polymyositis may also have the dry eyes and mouth of Sjögren's syndrome (Key 17).

Treatment: Doctors can set up a treatment program to minimize damage and alleviate symptoms. Treatment consists of a combination of the following: exercise (Keys 21 and 32), corticosteroids, most commonly prednisone (Key 29), immunosuppressive drugs (Key 28), physical therapy (Key 43) and rest (Key 35). A controversial new technique that may prove effective against myositis is plasmapheresis, in which the patient's blood is removed and treated to remove substances that may contribute to muscle weakness.

15

OSTEOPOROSIS

What is osteoporosis? Osteoporosis, or porous bone, is an age-related condition in which bone mass decreases, causing bones to fracture easily. As many as 15 to 20 million Americans have the disease. According to the National Institutes on Health, about 1.3 million fractures caused by osteoporosis occur every year to those over age 45; among those who live to be 90, one third of women and one sixth of men will fracture a hip.

Rheumatologist Dr. Lawrence Shulman emphasizes that prevention is the key to decreasing these statistics. "We have to be sure that we build up as much bone as possible in early life and that we lose as little as possible after mid-life," says Shulman. "We need to put some bone reserves in the bank."

Where does osteoporosis strike? Any bone can fracture because of osteoporosis. However, the most common sites are the vertebral spinal column, the wrist, and the hip. Twelve to 20 percent of older people with hip fracture die within a year after the fracture.

Who develops osteoporosis? If you are a woman and are thin, small-boned, white, and postmenopausal, you are at high risk for developing osteoporosis. There are a number of identifiable factors for developing osteoporosis:

- *Age*. The likelihood of developing osteoporosis increases with age.
- *Sex*. Women are six to eight times more likely to develop the condition than men.

- *Early or surgical menopause.* A sudden drop in estrogen is associated with an increased risk for osteoporosis.
- *Race.* Whites are more likely to develop the condition than blacks. In fact, on average, blacks have 10 percent more bone mass than whites.
- *Low calcium intake.*
- *Lack of weight-bearing exercise.*
- *Being underweight.*
- *A family history* of the condition.
- *Cigarette smoking.*
- *Excessive use of cortisone-type drugs* such as prednisone.

What causes osteoporosis? The disease results from loss of bone mass, causing the bones to fracture easily.

Is there a cure for osteoporosis? There is no known cure, but extensive research in osteoporosis is taking place.

Symptoms: Unfortunately, osteoporosis does not show up until significant bone loss has taken place. Often it goes undetected until a fracture occurs.

Diagnosis: Two common diagnostic techniques are photon absorptiometry, which is used to measure bone density, and computerized tomography (CT), which uses x-rays to create a three-dimensional image. Unfortunately, bone loss cannot be determined until 30 percent of bone density has been lost.

Treatment: A major treatment for women is estrogen therapy, which slows bone loss and prevents fractures. It is important to start taking estrogen right after menopause. However, the treatment is effective if begun as late as 10 to 15 years after menopause.

Both older men and women should take a minimum of 1,200 to 1,500 milligrams of calcium a day, equivalent to four or five eight-ounce glasses of milk. Other sources of calcium are yogurt, cheese, salmon, canned sardines, oysters, shrimp, dried beans, and dark green vegetables. Because calcium supplements are often not absorbed sufficiently by the body, it is preferable to eat calcium-rich foods rather than taking calcium tablets. However, if you can not tolerate dairy products and must take your calcium through supplements, calcium citrate appears to be the best option.

Excessive dietary fat and protein in the diet should be avoided, as they interfere with calcium absorption. In addition, vitamin D is necessary for calcium absorption. Normal healthy adults who are outdoors every day for about 30 minutes do not need to take vitamin D supplements.[7] However, those who are not should take 400 to 800 IUs a day.

Studies have shown that lack of exercise results in bone loss. The National Institutes on Health recommend a program of moderate weight-bearing exercise, such as brisk walking, running, tennis, or aerobic dance (Key 32), three to four hours a week. Non-weight bearing exercise such as swimming is not as effective.

Finally, the drug etridonate has been found to be very effective at retarding loss of bone mass. However, at this writing it has not been approved to treat osteoporosis.

[7]Karyn Holm and Jane Walker, *Geriatric Nursing,* May/June 1990, pp. 141–142.

16

PAGET'S DISEASE

What is Paget's disease of bone? Paget's disease of bone,[8] also known as osteitis deformans, is a chronic disorder in which bone formation, which occurs throughout life, is speeded up, causing a change in the strength and shape of the bone. It was first described by English surgeon John Paget in 1877. However, evidence of the disease has been found in an Egyptian mummy.

In Paget's disease of the bone, affected areas become thicker and softer than normal, and weight-bearing bones actually bend. According to the Arthritis Foundation, "Bone is made . . . in a jumbled fashion. It is disorganized, bulky, has extra blood vessels, and is somewhat softer than normal bone. X-rays will show a 'cottonball' puffiness on the bone. Abnormal bone formation may occur for 20 years while the disease is active."

Where does Paget's disease strike? The areas most commonly affected are the pelvis, the lower back, the tailbone, the skull, and the long bones in the legs. It does not spread from one area to another but usually settles in one or more specific section of bone, leaving the rest of the skeleton untouched. Joints near the affected area may also be involved. Rarely, Paget's may affect other areas of the body; for example, elderly persons may develop congestive heart failure if the

---

[8]Paget's disease actually describes two disorders—Paget's disease of bone and Paget's disease of the skin. This key covers Paget's disease of the bone only.

heart becomes overworked from pumping more blood through extra blood vessels that have formed in "pagetic" bone. Muscle and sensory disturbances may also occur, such as difficulties in vision, swallowing, balance, or speech. Some victims also get gout or pseudogout. In rare cases a bone tumor can occur.

Who develops Paget's disease? Paget's disease is an age-related disorder, frequently striking between the ages of 50 and 70. Some experts assert that it is slightly more common in men than women. As many as three million Americans over the age of 40 have "pagetic" bone, and one in 10 older adults over age 80 have the disease. It is common in English-speaking countries and rare in China, Japan, India, and Scandinavian countries, suggesting an environmental cause. People of western European ancestry are most likely to develop the disease. There is a tendency for Paget's disease to run in families.

What causes Paget's disease? The cause is not known, but there is a theory that it is caused by a viral infection contracted many years before symptoms develop.

Is there a cure for Paget's disease? There is no cure, but the disease can be successfully treated if caught early enough. Eventually Paget's disease wears itself out and symptoms may wax and wane, but any bone alteration remains, so that, for example, the skull may be permanently enlarged or the legs may remain bowed.

Symptoms: The majority of people with Paget's disease are symptom-free. Those who do have symptoms report a range of problems. Very often the condition is not diagnosed until a doctor finds evidence of the disease when a bone X-ray is taken for another reason. When symptoms are evident, the most common manifestation of the disease is "deep bone" pain and "warmth" over the affected area. If skull bone is affected, headaches may occur. Bones may also break or fracture, the legs may become bowed, or the spine may be bent forward. Hearing may also be affected, with ringing in the ears or a hearing loss. Sciatica, (severe pain in the lower back, down the back of the thighs and buttocks and into the legs) may also occur.

Diagnosis: Diagnosis is made by X-ray, sometimes by bone scans, and infrequently by bone biopsies. Physicians also test the patient's blood and urine for excess products of bone breakdown or buildup.

Treatment: Treatment consists of a combination of the following: pain relief (Key 27) and drugs to slow down or block the rate of bone breakdown, perhaps including calcitonin, a natural hormone that reduces breakdown of blood, and diphosphonates, which slows breakdown and formation of blood. Another commonly used medicine is etridonate, which may actually increase bone mass (Key 31). Occasionally, surgery is required for a hip replacement or to reduce hearing loss. Victims should avoid obesity, which adds stress to the bones and joints. Shoe lifts may be useful for bowed legs, canes for walking, and hearing aids if the ear is affected. Finally, exercise is vital to healthy bones.

17

SJÖGREN'S SYNDROME

What is Sjögren's syndrome, and where does it strike? If you have a dry mouth and difficulty in chewing, swallowing, and speaking, you may have Sjögren's. Sjögren's is a disorder that often accompanies rheumatoid arthritis, systemic lupus erythematosus, scleroderma, and polymyositis. It causes dry eyes and a dry mouth.

Who develops Sjögren's syndrome? It is found most often in women who have passed menopause. It affects more than a million people in the United States.

What causes Sjögren's syndrome? Sjögren's is an immune system disorder which leads to the excessive production of white blood cells, called lymphocytes. These blood cells can destroy the tear and salivary glands and also lead to the production of substances called autoantibodies that damage the glands. Other parts of the body may also be affected.

Is there a cure? There is no cure, but symptoms can be greatly relieved with treatment.

Symptoms: Symptoms vary greatly according to the individual. However, the most common characteristic of Sjögren's is a dry mouth and difficulty in chewing, swallowing, and speaking. Other symptoms include red, itchy eyes; a dry, cracked tongue; and swollen lymph glands. According to the Arthritis Foundation, about half of all victims have swollen salivary glands and fever. Dental cavities occur frequently. Rarely, victims develop cancer of the lymph tissue.

Diagnosis: To diagnose dryness of the eye, physicians may perform a Schirmer test in which filter paper is placed under the eyelid. Eye doctors also test the cornea with a dye that stains only dry areas. A special kind of X-ray called a sialogram may also be performed to test the salivary glands, and a lip biopsy may be performed. A urine test may be necessary to detect kidney involvement.

Treatment: Treatment for dry eyes includes the use of artificial tears and eye drops and special treatments for use while sleeping. Patients with dry mouths are advised to drink fluids, use mouth rinses, and suck lozenges. Humidifiers and moisturizers help dry skin, and lubricants can help vaginal dryness for women. In addition, taking aspirin (Key 24) and corticosteroid drugs (Key 29) may help arthritis symptoms. And, of course, exercise is important (Keys 21 and 32). For information about the best products on the market for treating Sjögren's, contact the "Moisture Seekers," whose address is listed in Key 49.

18

RAYNAUD'S PHENOMENON

What is Raynaud's phenomenon, and where does it strike? If your hands turn purple whenever you are in cold temperatures, you may have Raynaud's phenomenon, or Raynaud's disease. Raynaud's is a condition in which poor blood flow occurs in the hands, toes, ears, or tip of the nose when they are exposed to the cold or when the individual is under emotional stress. The skin may appear white, blue, purple, or red. The affected part may be easily damaged by the cold. In addition, victims tend to have cold hands and feet even in warm temperatures.

Raynaud's sometimes occurs with rheumatic conditions, including rheumatoid arthritis and SLE. Virtually all people who have scleroderma have Raynaud's. When the condition accompanies another disease, it is called Raynaud's phenomenon; when it occurs alone, it is called Raynaud's disease.

Raynaud's sometimes behaves differently for older adults, in whom symptoms may occur even though temperatures are not significantly low.

What is the cause of Raynaud's? The cause of Raynaud's is not known, although there is evidence that the autonomic nervous system of sufferers responds too quickly to cold. The condition usually begins between the ages of 20 and 40 and is more common in women than men.

Treatment: The object of treatment is to avoid cold and emotional stress and to prevent damage if it occurs. It is important to keep your body warm, taking such measures as dressing warmly, keeping the rooms in your house warm, and avoiding cold water or cold objects. In addition, use lotion frequently and mild soaps to treat dry skin.

A new therapy developed at the U.S. Army Research Institute of Environmental Medicine and the Lahey Clinic Medical Center in Massachusetts can be done at home. Patients are advised to sit in a cold room with their hands in warm water for at least ten minutes; their symptoms will lessen. Patients may have to experiment with the procedure for a while to discover how often they need to use it to cut down on symptoms.

If you have Raynaud's, you should not smoke and should not take drugs that constrict blood vessels, such as beta blockers and some cold tablets.

19

BURSITIS AND TENDONITIS

What are bursitis and tendonitis? Both bursitis and tendonitis are painful localized inflammations that usually start suddenly, are short term, and do not permanently damage tissue. Specifically, bursitis is inflammation of the bursa, a fluid-filled sac found near joints that minimizes friction between muscles. If a bursa is irritated or injured, the sac becomes inflamed and fills with fluid. Tendonitis is inflammation of the tendons, bands of fibrous tissue connecting muscles to bones.

Where do bursitis and tendonitis strike? They usually occur in the shoulder, elbow, hand, hip, knee, or ankle. Examples are:

- tennis elbow—outside of the elbow.
- golfer's elbow—inside of the elbow.
- trigger finger—tendons that move the fingers.
- deQuervain's tendonitis—wrist and base of the thumb.
- weaver's bottom—bottom of the pelvis.
- housemaid's knee—front of the kneecap.
- trochanteric bursitis—outer side of the hip.
- anserine bursitis—inside of the knees.

Who develops tendonitis and bursitis, and what causes them? Both conditions can occur in individuals who use repeated motion. There's even a new classification called "video game finger," caused by repeated stress to finger joints.

Is there a cure for bursitis and tendonitis? The course

of both conditions is short term, and they do not cause permanent damage.

Symptoms: Bursitis usually causes acute pain, while tendonitis generates a dull ache that worsens with movement. However, a milder form of bursitis, chronic or subacute bursitis, can mimic tendonitis and is difficult to distinguish on the basis of the type of pain alone.

Treatment: If the factors that caused the tendonitis or bursitis are eliminated, the condition will usually go away. Physicians can reduce the swelling of bursitis by drawing off fluid with a syringe and prescribing anti-inflammatory drugs.

If bursitis comes back in the same spot, a doctor can surgically remove the offending bursa. Bursae that are difficult to reach can be injected with steroids and a local anesthetic.

20

OTHER FORMS OF ARTHRITIS

The conditions in this section are either forms of arthritis or are problems that can occur with arthritis.

Bunions: A bunion is inflammation, swelling, and a bony, fibrous bump on the outside edge of the joint at the base of the toe. People who develop bunions usually have a minor foot disorder in which the big toe overlaps one or more other toes (*hallus valgus*). The condition is inherited or congenital. Poorly fitted shoes that squeeze toes together contribute to the problem. Three times as many women as men have bunions.

The symptoms of bunions are impossible to miss. They include a big toe that overlaps one or more other toes, thickened skin over a bump at the base of the toe, foot pain, and stiffness. Sometimes fluid accumulates under the bump at the base of the toe. Bunions are curable with treatment, and preventive measures can eliminate reoccurrences.

Bunions are sometimes treated with injections of certain drugs and whirlpool baths. Home treatment should include separating the big toe from the others with a foam rubber pad, wearing a protective pad over the bunion, and using arch supports. A procedure called a bunionectomy may be necessary. The surgery can be performed by a general surgeon, orthopedist, or podiatrist (Keys 22 and 40).

Carpal tunnel syndrome: Carpal tunnel syndrome is a painful condition caused by pressure on the median nerve at the wrist, which travels through a narrow canal called the carpal tunnel. Its symptoms are pain, tingling, and numbness in the thumb, index, middle, and ring fingers and, sometimes, the shoulder. Symptoms frequently worsen at night, and you may awaken with pain. The syndrome can result in permanent nerve and muscle damage if not treated. However, if treatment begins early enough in the process, there is a good chance the condition will heal.

Any activity that causes the wrist to be bent forward can cause or aggravate the condition. Other possible causes are rheumatoid arthritis and thyroid disease. Carpal tunnel syndrome may be treated with splints, nonsteroidal anti-inflammatory drugs, steroid injections, and surgery.

Inflammatory bowel disease and associated arthritis: Inflammation of the bowels is called inflammatory bowel disease (IBD). IBD is actually a combination of Crohn's disease (ulcers and inflammation of any part of the digestive tract from the mouth to anus) and ulcerative colitis (ulcers and inflammation on the lining of the colon). People with the latter may also develop ankylosing spondylitis, a form of arthritis that attacks the spine. About one in four persons with IBD also develops symptoms of arthritis.

IBD can occur at any age, but it is most common in the middle years. It does not favor either sex. A faulty immune system is a suspected cause of the disease.

Symptoms for ulcerative colitis are rectal bleeding, abdominal cramping, weight loss, and fever. In addition, about one fourth of IBD victims have a painful skin rash (erythema nodosum) on the lower legs. The disease is generally most active when the colon is inflamed, and the intensity of the symptoms depend on the extent of the disease. The symptoms of Crohn's disease are fever, weight loss, and loss of appetite. Arthritis symptoms associated with both diseases attack the large joints. A small number of Crohn's disease victims have inflammation of the sacroiliac or spine.

Physicians prescribe a variety of medications to treat IBD. They include sulfasalazine, a sulfa drug that helps to retard both the bowel disease and the arthritis symptoms; corticosteroids (Key 29); immunosuppressives (Key 28); and nonsteroidal anti-inflammatory drugs (Key 26). Other forms of treatment include exercise (Keys 21 and 32), surgery (Key 40), and diet (Key 33).

Osteonecrosis: Osteonecrosis means "death of bone." In this condition, bone is weakened by a lack of blood supply to the area and eventually develops small breaks. Osteonecrosis frequently strikes the hips, knees, and shoulders and can involve more than one joint.

According to the Arthritis Foundation, the following groups are most at risk for developing osteonecrosis:
• people with rheumatic diseases such as rheumatoid arthritis.
• people who are taking steroids.
• alcoholics.
• scuba divers who have had the bends.
Osteonecrosis of the knee occurs most often between the ages of 50 and 60.

The lack of blood supply that causes osteonecrosis may in turn be caused by a number of things, ranging from alcoholism to an infection. Symptoms include pain, limited joint motion, muscle spasm, and joint stiffness.

Treatment of osteonecrosis is very important to prevent increasing bone damage. It includes aspirin (Key 24), other nonsteroidal anti-inflammatory drugs (Key 26), heat (Key 34), and joint replacement surgery (Key 40).

Psoriatric arthritis: This type of arthritis is a sometime companion to a skin disease called psoriasis. It is only rarely severe. Psoriatric arthritis usually affects the small joints of the fingers and toes. Sometimes the spine is affected. The appendages and nails may become deformed. Treating psoriatric arthritis requires treating the skin disease and the arthritis symptoms separately.

TMJ syndrome: TMJ is an abbreviation for temporomandibular joint, the technical term for the jaw. TMJ syndrome occurs when the jaw doesn't perform properly, resulting in tenderness, pain when chewing or yawning, a clicking sound when using the mouth, and locking of the jaw. Less common symptoms are headache, earache, and dizziness. The syndrome can be caused by any condition that irritates the jaw, including arthritis, clenching and grinding of the teeth, and misalignment in the jaw. In order to treat the syndrome, the aggravating condition and pain must be treated.

Vasculitis: Vasculitis is a group of diseases distinguished by inflammation of the blood vessels. The following list includes those vasculitides that affect older persons.

Vasculitis in arthritis. This vasculitis, which is characterized by skin blotches and sores, accompanies other forms of arthritis. It can affect the central nervous system of people with lupus. The disease is treated with corticosteroids (Key 29) and immunosuppressive drugs.

Polyarteritis. This rare disease involves the inflammation of many (poly) blood vessels. It affects primarily men over the age of 45. It is often diagnosed through an angiogram and biopsy and is treated with steroids (Key 29).

Hypersensitivity vasculitis. This is the most common form of vasculitis, affecting people of any age. Symptoms may be short-term or chronic and include skin eruptions, fever, loss of appetite, and fatigue. Diagnosis is made through a biopsy, and steroid creams are used for treatment (Key 29).

Wegener's granulomatosis. Named after the physician who first identified it, this type of vasculitis involves the formation of inflamed growths within blood vessels. It commonly affects men over the age of 40. Symptoms include bleeding from the nose, inflammation of the nostrils and throat, and pain in the sinuses and ears. Diagnosis is made through biopsy of the skin. If Wegener's granulomatosis goes untreated, it can seriously damage the kidneys and lungs. Before the development of steroids and immunosuppressive treatments, the disease was fatal (Keys 28 and 29).

21

TIPS FOR PREVENTING AND LESSENING THE COURSE OF ARTHRITIS: A CONVERSATION WITH DR. ARTHUR GRAYZEL

At present there are no known ways to prevent inflammatory conditions such as rheumatoid arthritis. However, there are specific measures that you can take to prevent the noninflammatory forms of arthritis such as osteoarthritis, as well as to retard their progress. The following tips were provided by Dr. Arthur Grayzel, senior vice president, medical affairs of the Arthritis Foundation.

According to Dr. Grayzel, older people should *actively* participate in a program designed to increase elasticity of the tissues surrounding the joints. Three of the elements in the program involve exercise. To put it simply, *not* exercising has severe consequences. Joints become stiff, and muscles shrink and weaken. In addition, joints that are never moved can become locked, resulting in deformity.

Here are the measures recommended by Dr. Grayzel. Instruction for these exercises can be obtained from chapters of the Arthritis Foundation and from physical and occupational therapists.

Range-of-motion exercises: The first element of the program is to put your joints through their range of motion every day (Figure 21-1). In younger people, everyday activities such as lifting and walking usually accomplish these motions automatically. As people age, these activities are curtailed. At that time, according to Dr. Grayzel, "it's a good idea to do specific, *regular and complete* range-of-motion exercises."

There are two ways to do range-of-motion exercises: actively, through using your own muscle strength, or passively, with someone assisting you. Dr. Grayzel emphasizes that it is best to do the exercises actively if at all possible.

Range-of-motion exercises are *not* exercises as most of us usually think of them. The purpose is to maintain free joint motion, not to build strength. They are gentle exercises that can be done very simply and don't have to be very repetitive. And they can save joints.

Many people find that these exercises are easier to do in warm water. The warmth of the water is soothing, and its buoyancy is important for people who are losing some strength. The Arthritis Foundation's aquatic program is designed specifically to fill this need; local YMCAs frequently offer similar aquatic exercise programs.

Stretching: The second element is to *stretch*. There are very simple and gentle stretching exercises that maintain the length of muscles and help joint motion.

Muscle strengthening: The third element is to do muscle strengthening exercises. Dr. Grayzel points out that one of the interesting advances in recent years is the demonstration that such exercises are effective in older people. Muscle strengthening exercises include very general restrictive activities such as weight-lifting. These exercises enable you to walk better and perform your daily activities better. If you don't do them, there is a good chance that your muscles will weaken. Older people should do these exercises under supervision or with guidance.

Avoid injury: This measure applies to people of any

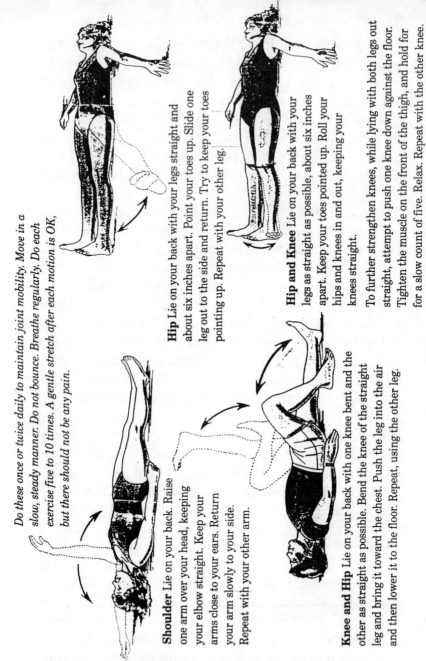

Do these once or twice daily to maintain joint mobility. Move in a slow, steady manner. Do not bounce. Breathe regularly. Do each exercise five to 10 times. A gentle stretch after each motion is OK, but there should not be any pain.

Shoulder Lie on your back. Raise one arm over your head, keeping your elbow straight. Keep your arms close to your ears. Return your arm slowly to your side. Repeat with your other arm.

Knee and Hip Lie on your back with one knee bent and the other as straight as possible. Bend the knee of the straight leg and bring it toward the chest. Push the leg into the air and then lower it to the floor. Repeat, using the other leg.

Hip Lie on your back with your legs straight and about six inches apart. Point your toes up. Slide one leg out to the side and return. Try to keep your toes pointing up. Repeat with your other leg.

Hip and Knee Lie on your back with your legs as straight as possible, about six inches apart. Keep your toes pointed up. Roll your hips and knees in and out, keeping your knees straight.

To further strengthen knees, while lying with both legs out straight, attempt to push one knee down against the floor. Tighten the muscle on the front of the thigh, and hold for for a slow count of five. Relax. Repeat with the other knee.

Figure 21–1: SAMPLE RANGE-OF-MOTION EXERCISES

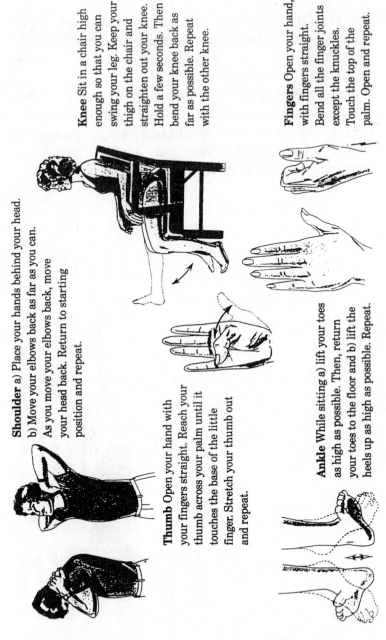

Shoulder a) Place your hands behind your head. b) Move your elbows back as far as you can. As you move your elbows back, move your head back. Return to starting position and repeat.

Knee Sit in a chair high enough so that you can swing your leg. Keep your thigh on the chair and straighten out your knee. Hold a few seconds. Then bend your knee back as far as possible. Repeat with the other knee.

Fingers Open your hand, with fingers straight. Bend all the finger joints except the knuckles. Touch the top of the palm. Open and repeat.

Thumb Open your hand with your fingers straight. Reach your thumb across your palm until it touches the base of the little finger. Stretch your thumb out and repeat.

Ankle While sitting a) lift your toes as high as possible. Then, return your toes to the floor and b) lift the heels up as high as possible. Repeat.

Courtesy of the Arthritis Foundation, *Exercise and Your Arthritis*, 1986.

age. Dr. Grayzel advises that people need to take injury to joints very seriously and to make sure that they carry out rehabilitation afterwards, because injury is a major cause of arthritis later in life.

Lose excess weight: Excess weight places tremendous strain on joints. According to Dr. Grayzel, anyone who is 20 percent over "ideal" body weight should lose weight. (To determine your ideal body weight, check with your physician or physical therapist.)

22

MEDICAL CARE PROVIDERS FOR ARTHRITIS PATIENTS

The primary rule for general medical care, including treatment of arthritis symptoms, is to find one primary physician that you can grow older with. The great majority of older adults with arthritis do not need a medical specialist, such as a rheumatologist or orthopedist. They need a reliable physician who can handle all of their medical needs. As Kate Lorig and James F. Fries point out in *The Arthritis Helpbook,* "The fewer doctors you have, the better coordinated your health care will be."

There are three types of primary physicians from which to choose: *internists, family practitioners* (also called general practitioners), and *geriatricians.* Internists are medical doctors (M.D.s) who specialize in the diagnosis and medical treatment of disease in adults. Family practitioners are M.D.s who specialize in providing comprehensive health care for all members of a family, regardless of age or sex, on a continuing basis. However, if one is available, a geriatrician is the best choice. Geriatricians are M.D.s, but they are not medical specialists like internists or family practitioners. They have had special training in geriatrics—the study of the care of the aged. *The services of all three types of physicians are covered by Medicare.* Local offices on aging (listed in the yellow pages under Aging, Elderly, or Aged) have lists of geriatricians working in the community.

To check the credentials of a doctor in your area, the American Board of Medical Specialties has a hotline for consumers seeking answers to questions about a doctor's area of specialty and board-certification. The number is (800) 776-CERT.

Relating to your doctor: The following excerpt from the Arthritis Foundation's public information materials on relating to physicians offers important advice on patient/doctor relationships:

In order to be more at ease with both your doctor and other health professionals, try to realize that they are human beings too. Like you, they are subject to moods, pressures, and mistakes. There is no reason to be in awe of your doctor, nor is there any need to blindly follow orders without asking questions.

If you tend to hold your doctor in awe, as many people do, you may not want to bother him or her with questions. If you feel this way, try to remember that your doctor's job is to provide you with good medical care. Therefore, you have the right to receive certain services from your doctor.

Doctors aren't mind readers or magicians. Most of the information doctors use to diagnose and treat you must come from you. Therefore, your doctor *needs* your ideas and observations. It's in your best interests to be specific about how you feel and what you think.

Also, if your doctor explains something to you and you don't understand it, he or she won't know that until you say so. You might tell the doctor: "I still don't understand. Can you explain it again?" Don't feel stupid if you have to ask the same question again. Part of a doctor's job is to be an "educator," and this often means going over the same point several times.[9]

When it comes to arthritis treatment, a good physician will provide the facts about your disease and the proper treatment. This should include information, in language that you and other health consumers can understand, on what to expect from the disease process, as well as facts about the medications being prescribed—their cost, possible side effects, instructions on how to take them, and other possible options. Two other areas that should be covered when relevant are any risks from the diagnostic tests being done and what portion of the treatment is covered by Medicare and other health insurance.

Before visiting your doctor, you should prepare to make the most out of the limited time most physicians have to spend with their patients. Here are some tips:

- Before the visit, write down all questions you may have.
- Take along a complete record of all prescribed medications, over-the-counter drugs, and vitamins you are taking.
- Be honest about your symptoms and any problems you are having with your treatment.
- Describe any pain you are having as clearly as possible, including the location and intensity. It will help your doctor if you can tell him how intense the pain is on a scale of 1 to 10.
- Describe any limitations you may be experiencing, such as problems driving or walking.
- Make notes or use a tape recorder during your visit to make sure that you don't forget important things

---

[9]*Help Your Doctor—Help Yourself,* Arthritis Foundation, 1988, p. 4.

that you and your doctor discuss about your condition and its treatment.

Rheumatologists and orthopedic surgeons: Specialists, particularly rheumatologists and orthopedic surgeons, come into the picture for arthritis sufferers who have severe or complicated cases. Rheumatology became a specialty of internal medicine in 1940 to treat the medical aspects of arthritis-related disease. When surgery is required, the rheumatologist will refer the patient to an orthopedic surgeon. State chapters of the Arthritis Foundation have lists of local rheumatologists and orthopedists (Key 48). (For more information on choosing surgeons, see below.)

Chiropractors, podiatrists, and physiatrists: Chiropractors, podiatrists, and physiatrists also treat arthritis-related problems. Chiropractors are not medical doctors; they manipulate the spine to restore normal functioning. Medicare pays only for the manual manipulation of the spine to correct a specific problem that can be demonstrated by X-ray. However, Medicare will not pay for the diagnostic or therapeutic services of a chiropractor.

Podiatrists diagnose, treat, and prevent diseases and injuries of the foot. They may do surgery, make devices to correct or prevent foot problems, provide toenail care, and prescribe certain drugs. *A podiatrist is not licensed to treat diseases or injuries of any other part of the body.* Podiatrists complete four years of professional school; once they have been licensed, Medicare will cover the cost of their services except routine foot care. (However, routine foot care is covered if it is required by complications of diabetes.)

Physiatrists are doctors whose specialty is physical medicine, including rehabilitation and physical therapy. Medicare covers the cost of their services.

Other health professionals: Other health professionals central to the treatment of arthritis include registered nurses, dieticians, physical therapists, occupational therapists, pharmacists, and homemaker/home-health aides.

Nurses trained in the care of arthritis patients assist doctors and patients with treatment. They are an invaluable source for answers to questions and explanations of the whys and wherefores of treatment programs. Under very limited circumstances Medicare will pay some of the costs of their services when prescribed by a physician.

Registered dieticians provide nutritional care and dietary counseling. Unfortunately, Medicare generally will not pay for a dietician's services.

Physical therapists help people whose strength, ability to move, sensation, or range of motion is impaired. They may use exercise; heat, cold, or water therapy; or other treatments to control pain, strengthen muscles, and improve coordination. All physical therapists complete a program leading to a bachelor's degree, and some of them receive postgraduate training. Medicare will pay some of the costs of outpatient treatments when prescribed by a physician. Physical therapy performed in a hospital or skilled nursing facility is covered by Medicare.

Occupational therapists assist patients with handicaps to function more independently. They may provide exercise programs; heat, cold, and whirlpool treatments to relieve pain; and splints and adaptive equipment to improve function and independence. The costs of occupational therapy will be paid in part by Medicare if the patient is referred as an outpatient by a doctor or in full if the patient is in a hospital or skilled nursing facility.

Homemaker/home-health aides provide personal care such as assistance in bathing, grooming, dressing, cooking, and cleaning under the supervision of a professional person. Standards for these services are set by the National Council for Homemaker-Home Health Aide Services. Medicare will cover these services only under very limited circumstances.

Pharmacists fill prescriptions for medications and are an excellent source for information on side effects and interactions of drugs, including those sold over the counter.

Finally, *social workers*, *information* and *referral specialists,* state Arthritis Foundation chapters, and local organizations for the aging are important sources of information on how to locate needed medical programs and services.

23

TREATMENT

The rule of thumb for treating arthritis is that each treatment plan is unique to the individual's type of condition and situation. However, there are a number of treatment basics with which many arthritis sufferers will become acquainted. They include medication, exercise, rest, physical and occupational therapy, diet, pain management, joint protection, surgery, adapting to limitations, and taking part in support groups and counseling. All of these are covered in depth in separate Keys in this book, but they are so vital to living with the symptoms of arthritis that we have chosen to list them here to get the "big picture" of what can be done to treat these conditions.

The treatment plan: When arthritis is moderate to severe, the physicians will set up a treatment plan geared to the individual. The plan may include a range of health professionals. It may require adjustments in medication over time and will undoubtedly change as the condition improves or worsens. Of course, it will also vary according to the type of arthritis that is causing the symptoms.

It is very important to stick to the plan that the doctor prescribes. *Never* change your treatment plan without talking to your doctor first. For example, the drugs that the physician prescribes may take time to work. Some drugs even take months before the effects show. Do not stop your medication on your own!

Medication: Medications that treat arthritis and other diseases that commonly strike older persons are big business. The Pharmaceutical Manufacturers Association estimates that half of its $8.2 billion research and development budget goes to developing medications that will benefit older adults for such diseases as arthritis. At last count 259 such medications were in development in human trials or awaiting approval by the Food and Drug Administration.[10]

The medications that are used for arthritis treatment range from the best health consumer bargain in the world, aspirin tablets, to the new wonder drug for severe cases of arthritis, methotrexate. The medications prescribed for most, but not all, types of arthritis fall into two categories—those that relieve pain and/or reduce inflammation and those that modify the progression of the disease. (For a comprehensive look at the range of medicines used for arthritis treatment, see Keys 24 to 31. If a specific drug is not listed in one of these Keys, look in the Key that discusses the disease that it is commonly prescribed to treat.)

It's important to remember that drugs act differently in older people than in the young, making unusual reactions more likely with increasing age. In addition, most older people take a number of medications at the same time. In fact, the average number of drugs that people over 60 take annually is six.[11] And just two drugs can interact and cause significant problems. Therefore it is very important you give *all physicians* that you see complete records of *all medications* that you are taking, including over-the-counter drugs and vitamins.

Finding the right drug or combination of drugs for arthritis treatment is often a creative process and can

[10]"Scientific Frontier," *Arthritis Today,* May-June 1990, p. 10.
[11]Study by Pearl German at Johns Hopkins University, reported in National Institute on Aging, *Special Report, 1988,* p. 13.

be as frustrating as trying to create an oil painting with finger paints. There is no perfect drug that exactly fits the specifics of any particular type of arthritis. In addition, individuals react differently to medications; the anti-inflammatory drug that works for your neighbor may cause serious side effects for you.

Physicians also differ greatly in their preferred medicinal treatments for arthritis. One physician may push enteric coated aspirin to cut down on gastrointestinal problems, while another may be convinced that it is ineffective. In other words, it is important to understand that there are many approaches to treating arthritis with drugs and that your treatment plan may include trying a series of medications until you hit on the one that is right for you.

Exercise: Pulitzer-prize winning geriatrician Robert Butler says, "If exercise could be packed into a pill, it would be the single most widely prescribed, and beneficial, medicine in the nation." Regular exercise benefits the entire body, including the parts prone to arthritis. It can decrease many aspects of decline in physiological performance by ten to forty years. In fact, it can give a 70-year-old person the muscle capacity of a 30-year-old. As mentioned in Key 21, the types of exercise that are important for the prevention and reduction of arthritis symptoms are range-of-motion, strengthening, and stretching exercises. In addition, aerobic exercise is important for overall fitness.

Diet: While there is no diet that can "cure" arthritis, it is clear that certain conditions, such as gout and Sjögren's syndrome, benefit from specific regimens. When relevant, your doctor will recommend that you avoid certain foods. For more information on diet, see Key 33.

Weight control: According to Dr. David T. Felson at Boston City Hospital, "Obesity directly causes osteoarthritis in the knee and probably causes osteoarthritis in the back."[12] The link between obesity and osteoarthritis has been proven in a number of recent studies, including an analysis by Dr. Felson that showed that obesity at a young age can actually predict osteoarthritis at an older age. Another investigator found a similar relationship between gout and weight gain. Dr. Marc Hochberg at Johns Hopkins University found that weight gain, regardless of the weight at which the individual started out, could actually predict the occurrence of gout; every seven pounds of weight gain results in a 15 percent increase in the chance of developing gout.[13] If you are overweight, you should take off excess weight gradually but steadily in order to slow the disease process.

Rest: While exercise is vital to arthritis prevention, too much exercise can damage joints. Exercise steadied by rest is essential to healthy joints. In addition, rest becomes essential during times of arthritis flare-ups (Key 35).

Pain management: No one can say it more clearly than the Arthritis Foundation has in its pamphlet *Coping with Pain:* "Learning to cope with chronic (long-lasting) pain may be the toughest part of living with arthritis." However, there are a number of things that can be done to at least ease, if not erase, pain. These may include taking medications (Keys 24 to 31), applying heat and cold (Key 34), massage (Key 37), exercise (Keys 21 and 32), joint protection (Key 38), using splints (Key 39), surgery (Key 40), using transcutaneous electrical nerve stimulation (TENS) (Key 37), and re-

[12]Joseph Wallace, "Can Arthritis Be Prevented?" *Arthritis Today,* July-August 1990, p. 47.
[13]Ibid.

laxation techniques such as hypnosis and biofeedback (Key 35).

Joint protection: Learning how to protect joints is an important part of arthritis treatment. There are many things that can be done to reduce stress on joints while going about daily life, from applying splints to buying clothes with velcro fasteners. For detailed information on protecting joints, see Keys 38 and 39.

Surgery: When pain, deformity, and loss of function are severe, surgery may be required. Surgery may range from removing a diseased synovial membrane to replacing a hip. You may need to consider whether the surgery will be covered by Medicare, or, if you are not yet 65, by other health insurance. For detailed information on surgery for arthritis, see Key 40.

Adapting to limitations: There are many useful devices and services to which arthritis victims can turn, to ease the difficulty of getting around with a disability. Help ranges from the assistance of a home-health aide to adapting housing to be "user-friendly." For information on adjusting to limitations, see Keys 42 to 44.

24

ASPIRIN

Along with a tooth brush and comb, virtually every household medicine cabinet has a bottle of aspirin in it. Without question, aspirin is the most important drug in the world. This medicinal staple originated as a folk remedy when willow bark, which contains salicin, was used to reduce fevers in the mid 1700s.

Aspirin is a member of a family of drugs called salicylates. It is also one of the important nonsteroidal anti-inflammatory drugs (NSAIDS) that are so effective against the inflammation of arthritis. Technically called acetylsalicylic acid, aspirin works by suppressing the production of inflammation-producing fatty acids called prostaglandins which the body releases when cells are damaged. Aspirin also blocks pain. And, like all NSAIDS, it works quickly as a pain reliever.

Aspirin is such a powerful drug that it is often said that if it were introduced today, the Food and Drug Administration would not approve it as an over-the-counter medicine. Generally, physicians begin treatment of arthritis with aspirin therapy. Many of their patients feel dismayed at this, particularly after undergoing expensive diagnostic tests. They think that their doctor is not taking them seriously. However, aspirin is truly the drug of choice when it comes to arthritis symptoms.

Aspirin is not addictive, and it does not lose its effectiveness over time. A pain reliever at low doses, it becomes anti-inflammatory at higher doses. Joint inflammation responds slowly to aspirin. In arthritis with inflammation, the relief of symptoms may *not* seem as striking over time. Some brand names for aspirin are: Alka-Seltzer™, Anacin™, Aspergum™, Bayer™, BC Powder™, Bufferin™, Ecotrin™, Empirin™, Excedrin™, St. Joseph™, Vanquish™, and Zorprin™.

The pain relief and inflammation reduction benefit of aspirin is blessedly economical, making it an affordable treatment for many arthritis sufferers. Generic aspirin is as effective as brand-name aspirin, however the dosage should be checked to make sure that the necessary *amount* is being taken.

Side effects: Even though aspirin can be bought without a prescription, it can have serious side effects and should not be used on a self-prescribed basis. The most common side effect for aspirin is gastrointestinal problems, including nausea, vomiting, abdominal pain, black stools, heartburn, and indigestion. In addition, intestinal bleeding and ulcers may result. These complications are most common in people who regularly take large doses. The cause of these side effects is that the prostaglandins that aspirin eliminates not only cause inflammation but also protect the lining of the stomach.

Aspirin use can also cause a disturbing ringing in the ears (tinnitus) and hearing loss. For many, the ringing, while not pleasant, is worth the trade-off of reduced pain and inflammation. However, tinnitus is a sign of mild aspirin poisoning; this can be a problem for older people with a hearing impairment who may not hear the ringing and may be close to overdosing on the drug. Tinnitus is a temporary problem and, fortunately, stops when overuse of aspirin is stopped.

Aspirin can also interfere with proper nutrition, causing vitamin C excretion and folate deficiency. It can also interfere with blood clotting and can prevent the body from fighting off colds.

Allergic reactions: Individuals with an allergy to aspirin may experience a stuffy nose, skin rash, polyps in the nose, hives, and swelling of the tongue and lips. Rarely, allergic reactions may include liver irritation and kidney damage.

When *not* to take aspirin: Those who should use caution about taking aspirin are asthma sufferers, people with gastrointestinal problems, and those taking blood thinners.

How to take aspirin: There is no specific formula for taking the drug, but the rule is usually to take as much as can be tolerated. When inflammation is present, it is important to remember that the amount of aspirin needed is greater than the amount needed to reduce pain.

Because of the larger dose necessary to treat inflammation, aspirin can be purchased in extra-strength, time-released, and liquid form. The goal of aspirin treatment is to raise the dosage slowly to the maximum safe level. This optimizes its impact on inflammation. Unfortunately, the level at which aspirin is effective as an anti-inflammatory is also frequently the level which generally causes side effects—about 3.6 grams a day.[14]

Aspirin comes in grain or milligram (mg) tablets. "Adult strength" tablets are five grains or 325 milligrams (mg). For a "minor" headache the usual dosage is two adult tablets. This dosage also reduces fever. However, an individual with irritating rheumatoid arthritis symptoms may take up to 12 adult tablets a day; those with severe symptoms may take as many as 20 tablets.

A word of caution: Aspirin can decompose when frequently exposed to air. If you open an aspirin bottle and it smells like vinegar, discard the bottle.

---

[14]Judith K. Sands and Judith H. Mathews, *A Guide to Arthritis Home Health Care,* New York: John Wiley, 1988.

Cutting down on side effects: Aspirin should always be taken with food, milk, or an antacid to cut down on gastric side effects. Some physicians recommend taking coated aspirin (enteric aspirin) to cut down on gastrointestinal side effects. (Enteric aspirin bypasses the stomach and doesn't dissolve until it reaches the small intestine.) However, other doctors don't think that enteric aspirin is effective and don't recommend it. There is some indication that enteric aspirin is less effective for older persons, as well as for individuals taking medications. Some brand-names for coated aspirin are Ecotrin™, Easprin™, Encrapin™, and Cosprin™. Whether it cuts down on gastrointestinal problems or not, enteric aspirin takes longer to reach the blood stream and isn't useful for quick relief of pain and inflammation. Antacids cannot be used with enteric coated aspirin.

25

OTHER PAIN-RELIEVING DRUGS

Pain is nature's signal that something in the body is wrong. Pain occurs when the body's cells are injured and send a message to the brain that an assault has taken place. The message is never pleasant and is usually the major symptom that drives the afflicted to get help from a doctor.

Drugs that are used to stop pain are called analgesics. The previous chapter covered the analgesic most frequently called into action against pain—aspirin. Aspirin is particularly effective against rheumatoid arthritis because it not only helps to fight pain but also combats inflammation. However, aspirin can have serious side effects, and there are times when heavier hitters are needed against acute pain. This Key discusses the painkillers that physicians most often prescribe when acute pain is the only or major consideration. These drugs are for pain only; they don't help inflammation and are, therefore, not as effective for rheumatoid arthritis and other conditions involving inflammation.

The painkillers discussed here are not effective for long-term use. The body gets used to painkillers so that they may become less effective over time. This phenomenon is called tolerance; it means that the dosage has to be increased to get the same advantage.

There are two major types of analgesics—those that are not narcotic, such as aspirin, acetaminophen, and ibuprofen and those that are narcotic, such as Darvon™ (propoxyphene) and codeine. This Key covers a nonnarcotic alternative to aspirin, acetaminophen, and two frequently prescribed narcotic pain killers, Darvon™ and codeine. Other well-known narcotics, such as Percodan™ and Demerol™, are for temporary relief of severe pain such as that caused by a broken bone or fracture and are not appropriate for arthritis treatment.

Acetaminophen: When pain relief is the main goal and reduction of inflammation and redness is not a concern, acetaminophen may be a better alternative than aspirin or other drugs that are hard on the stomach. Some brand names for acetaminophen are Anacin-3™, Datril™, Dristan™, Excedrin™, Midol PMS™, Panadol™, Sinarest™, Sine-Aid™, Tylenol™, and Vanquish™. Like aspirin, acetaminophen is relatively inexpensive.

Acetaminophen is blessedly free of side effects. (However, any problems that do occur should be reported to a physician; for example, too much acetaminophen can damage the liver and kidneys.) In addition, acetaminophen is the only pain-reducing drug that is not addictive. The usual acetaminophen dosage for mild pain relief is two 10-grain tablets every four hours.

Propoxyphene: Propoxyphene is a narcotic that provides help against moderate pain. It is better known by the brand name Darvon Compound™ or Darvocet™. Darvon™ is used for the short-term relief of pain and is not effective against inflammation. It is not appropriate as part of a long-term treatment plan.

Darvon™ can cause sedation, drowsiness, dizziness, nausea, constipation, and skin rash. It may also cause a mentally dull feeling and, most seriously, has been implicated in suicides. Because Darvon™ is a narcotic, it can lead to addiction, with tolerance and dependence effects. It should *never* be taken with alcohol; the combination can cause serious central nervous system depression and has resulted in death. Darvon™ should be taken with food. It is more expensive than the safer alternative, acetaminophen.

Codeine: Like Darvon™, this narcotic pain reliever provides help against moderate pain. In the United States, it is usually sold under its generic name of codeine. Codeine is used for the short-term relief of pain and is not effective against inflammation. It is not appropriate as part of a long-term treatment plan. Side effects of codeine are similar to those for Darvon™. Codeine can interfere with medication taken for gout. It should be taken with food.

26

NONSTEROIDAL ANTI-INFLAMMATORY DRUGS

Two types of drugs work against inflammation—nonsteroidal anti-inflammatory drugs (NSAIDS) and corticosteroids. Of the two, NSAIDS are milder alternatives for long-term use. Aspirin is the best known and most popular NSAID, but many alternative NSAIDS are now available and more are coming on the market all the time.

More than 100 variations of NSAIDS are available internationally. They were developed in an attempt to find an inflammatory-reducing drug that would be easier than aspirin on the gastro-intestinal tract. Research has shown that NSAIDS reduce production of rheumatoid factor (Key 5). All NSAIDS work by blocking the production of prostaglandins, which protect the lining of the stomach. Therefore, gastrointestinal problems can occur.

Most NSAIDS require a prescription. The exceptions are aspirin and NSAIDS in the ibuprofen family. Many of the newer NSAIDS are as effective as aspirin, or more so. All NSAIDS relieve pain and reduce inflammation. However, they differ in chemical composition, and individual response is highly variable. You may have to try out different types until you find the one that works for you. In general terms, there is no evidence that one NSAID is more effective than another.

The *Merck Manual of Geriatrics,* a medical manual for physicians caring for older persons, asserts that the starting doses of NSAIDS should be lower for older people than younger persons.[15] Specifically, it recommends that patients start ibuprofen, the most popular non-aspirin NSAID, at 400 milligrams (mg) three or four times a day and then increase incrementally until side effects occur. As a general rule the maximum reasonable dose will be about 1½ to two times the starting dose.

Some NSAIDS are effective against pain and inflammation at relatively low doses, with the advantages of fewer side effects, greater economy, and greater convenience. Patience is required with NSAIDS. It takes two to three weeks for each drug to be effective.

Types of NSAIDS now available include the following: aspirin, diclofenac, diflunisal, fenoprofen, flurbiprofen, ibuprofen, indomethacin, ketoprofen, meclofenamate, mefenamic acid, naproxen, nonaspirin salicylates, phenylbutazone, piroxicam, sulindac, and tolmetin. Of these, ibuprofen is by far the most popular. Advil™ is the best known ibuprofen medication; others include Haltran™, Ibuprin™, Medipren™, Midol 200™, Motrin IB™, Nuprin™, Pamaprin IB™, Rufen™, and Trendar™.

NSAIDS that require a prescription are more expensive than those that can be bought over the counter. However, when comparing the costs of NSAIDS, the *dosage* should be evaluated rather than the number of tablets. Because it may take fewer tablets to reach a therapeutic level with a prescription drug, it may actually be less expensive than an over-the-counter drug. For example, ibuprofen, which can be purchased over the counter, comes in 200 mg tablets, whereas NSAIDS that require a prescription come in 400, 600, or 800 mg

---

[15]William B. Abrams and Robert Berkow, eds., *Merck Manual of Geriatrics,* Merck and Co., 1990, p. 110.

strengths, so it would take two, three, or four ibuprofen to equal one prescription NSAID tablet.

The side effects for different types of NSAIDS are similar. The most common, gastrointestinal upset, may mean that the drug has to be discontinued. This symptom appears to be worse during older age, and older persons with ulcer symptoms should be particularly careful about taking NSAIDS. Other side effects, which are far less common than stomach problems, include renal problems, anemia, water retention, headache, ringing in the ears, cognitive problems, hepatitis, hives, and shock. In addition, NSAIDS can contribute to the development of pneumonia.

Here are some tips for the effective use of NSAIDs:
- Always take with food or an antacid.
- Avoid other foods and drink that are irritating to the gastrointestinal tract.
- Cut down on salt, which can add to the tendency of NSAIDS to cause fluid retention.
- Call your doctor immediately if you notice the following: signs of blood in the urine or dark stools, a rash, rapid weight gain.

27

GOLD TREATMENTS AND PENICILLAMINE

Gold salts and penicillamine can be a boon for victims of rheumatoid arthritis who have exhausted every other option. Both drugs can actually cause remission. That's the good news. The bad news is that both can have serious side effects and should be tried only as a last resort.

Gold treatments: When gold treatments work for an individual, they can relieve the symptoms of rheumatoid arthritis, such as joint pain, joint stiffness, and inflammation. They can also prevent future damage. However, the down side is that they are not effective for everyone. According to the Arthritis Foundation, six in 10 people treated with gold in the early stages of the disease have good to excellent results—which, of course, means that four in 10 do not, either because of side effects or because the drug simply does not work for them.[16] And at least two recent studies have shed some doubt on the long-term effectiveness of the drug, although their results were controversial. One study found that gold capsules are effective at reducing rheumatoid arthritis but that another drug—methotrexate—is actually more effective, works more quickly, and has fewer side effects (Key 28).

Gold treatments have been used for rheumatoid arthritis for over 50 years. They are effective only against active inflammation; they can not undo damage that has

---

[16]Arthritis Foundation, *Gold Treatment: Information to Consider*, 1983, p. 3.

taken place previously. It is not clear how gold treatments work, but they appear to suppress the immune system and the production of damaging enzymes in the joints.

Gold salts are available in capsule form and by injection. There are distinct trade-offs for each. Capsules produce fewer side effects than injections but are less effective.

The technical name for the gold compounds that doctors use for injection are aurothioglucose and aurothiomalate. Their trade names are Solganal™ and Myochrisine™. The technical name for gold capsules is auranofin; the trade name is Ridaura™.

Physicians take a number of things into consideration before trying gold salts in any form, including:
- the number of affected joints.
- which joints are affected.
- the amount of damage as shown on X-rays.
- the treatment and response history.
- the stage of the disease process—whether it is too early or too late to begin treatment.

Gold salts work agonizingly slowly, which is often frustrating to the victim of rheumatoid arthritis. Because of the time that it takes for the medication to take effect, often 10 weeks, most physicians keep the patient on other forms of treatment until some improvement is demonstrated. Physicians also watch their patients on gold treatments closely, requiring regular blood and urine tests to reveal any liver damage, bone marrow problems, or kidney malfunction. Other side effects may include diarrhea for those taking the capsules, an itchy, scaly rash, and sores in the mouth.

Penicillamine: Penicillamine is not chemically related to gold salts. It does, however, have many similar properties, including the fact that it can effectively put the disease into remission. Unhappily, however, it is also similar to gold compounds in that side effects can be severe.

Penicillamine is available in capsules (Cuprimine™) or tablets (Depen™). Like gold salts, it works slowly, and the dosage is increased gradually over months. If the treatment is effective, doses are taken every day.

Penicillamine is only very distantly related to penicillin, and individuals who can not take the latter may be able to take the former. Its side effects are similar to those caused by gold salts. In addition, people taking this drug may lose their sense of taste or have an odd taste in the mouth.

28

METHOTREXATE AND OTHER IMMUNOSUPPRESSIVE DRUGS

Until recently, immunosuppressive drugs have been considered a bittersweet last resort for those who do not respond to other therapies and whose condition is severe and life-threatening. Developed to fight cancer, many of these drugs have side effects that can be *very risky,* including infection and, paradoxically, malignancy. However, one immunosuppressive drug, methotrexate (MTX), has been shown to produce dramatic results for arthritis sufferers and have fewer side effects than gold salts. Rheumatologist Dr. Lawrence Shulman calls the drug "unusually effective, according to most trials." And there is even more good news—it acts fast. MTX takes four to six weeks to work, compared to three or four months for compounds such as gold salts.

Immunosuppressive drugs, which were developed to use against tumors, work by decreasing the growth of rapidly producing cells. However, this process, which is essentially the poisoning of flourishing cells, is not selective; it ultimately affects the entire immune system, which can result in life-threatening problems.

There has been a great deal of concern about the use of these drugs because of their potentially toxic effects on the liver. However, according to Dr. Shulman, when methotrexate is given in low doses, the risk of liver toxicity "is quite small." He emphasizes that the dosage is an important factor and that most rheumatologists feel that the benefits outweigh the risks.

In general, all immunosuppressives can be used to treat a large number of arthritic conditions including rheumatoid arthritis, psoriatic arthritis, systemic lupus erythematosus, polymyositis, dermatomyositis, and some forms of vasculitis.

Side effects: Immunosuppressives share some serious side effects that can be fatal. Reactions can include bone marrow suppression, which results in problems in producing red and white blood cells and platelets; infections; and gastrointestinal problems. Physicians watch patients taking these medications very closely. If you are taking an immunosuppressive drug, your doctor will encourage you to take extraordinary care with your personal hygiene to avoid infection.

Methotrexate (MTX, Rheumatrex™): Methotrexate, which was discovered in 1949, is effective against leukemia in children and a rare cancer of the fetal membrane. It has been used successfully for rheumatoid arthritis, psoriatic arthritis, and dermatomyositis. Rheumatologists are currently debating when a patient should begin use of methotrexate. An article in *Geriatrics* magazine reported that some arthritis researchers believe that methotrexate should be used early in treatment, *before* joint damage or deformities occur.[17]

In addition to the side effects listed above for all immunosuppressive drugs, MTX can cause pulmonary problems, inflammation of the mucous membranes of the mouth, loss of hair, and hepatitis. However, side effects are far less common than those of other heavy-hitting antiarthritis drugs such as gold salts or penicil-

---

[17]Joel Kremer, "Severe rheumatoid arthritis: Current options in drug therapy," *Geriatrics,* December, 1990, p. 44.

lamine. They are also not prevalent at the low doses that are now being prescribed.

If you have trouble with methotrexate's side effects, folic acid may help. Researchers at the University of Alabama have found that a daily supplement of folic acid reduces toxicity for individuals taking the drug for rheumatoid arthritis. Folic acid is found in green, leafy vegetables and may be taken as a vitamin supplement.

Azathioprine (Imuran™): Imuran™ was developed to prevent transplant rejection and has been approved by the Food and Drug Administration for use against rheumatoid arthritis. It usually takes about three months to take effect. The drug is initially given in very high doses, at which time serious infection can develop. Doctors watch patients taking this drug very closely for signs of liver or kidney problems and tumors.

Cyclophosphamide (Cytoxan™): This drug has been used as an anticancer treatment for a long time. According to rheumatologist Dr. Shulman, it has been found to be very effective but too toxic to use in the treatment of arthritis. Cyclophosphamide is responsible for many of the side effects that are often associated with cancer treatment: nausea, vomiting, loss of appetite, and hair loss. Inflammation of the bladder is relatively common. Because the effects of this drug can be severe and dangerous, it is important to understand what to do if side effects occur. They require *immediate* medical attention. The Arthritis Foundation provides a list of side effects to watch for when taking this drug. If you are taking cyclophosphamide, you can request a copy from your closest Arthritis Foundation office.

29

CORTICOSTEROIDS

Corticosteroids are powerhouse drugs that can bring quick and dramatic relief during bouts of severe inflammation. In fact, they are the most effective drug available for reducing inflammation.

When corticosteroids are used on a long-term basis, they are given at low doses. According to rheumatologists Dr. Theodore Pincus and L.F. Callahan, "Doctors once discouraged the use of steroid drugs, primarily because of unacceptable side effects when given at high doses. With today's typical low doses, however, the side effects are minimal and may be acceptable to avoid progressive disease."[18]

Corticosteroids are used to treat severe inflammation from rheumatoid arthritis, dermatomyositis, vasculitis, systemic lupus erythematosus, scleroderma, and polymyalgia rheumatica. Corticosteroids are prescribed as pills, injections, eye drops, or creams. They should be taken with food to minimize gastrointestinal problems. Common corticosteroids are prednisone and methylprednisolone.

Corticosteroid injections: Physicians have injected corticosteroids directly into joints for many years to bring relief from severe inflammation. Importantly, far less of the drug gets into the system when it is injected directly into the joint than when it is taken as a pill. At least three months should elapse between injections, and the general rule is to wait as long as possible.

---

[18]Theodore Pincus and L. F. Callahan, "Remodeling the Pyramid," *Arthritis Today,* January-February 1991, p. 58.

Corticosteroid injections are most effective when they are first used. Welcome relief comes quickly and can last several months. However, over time, positive results subside and relief lasts only a couple of weeks. At this point physicians must be careful not to inject cortisone frequently into joints, as it can cause permanent damage if used too often. It is preferable to wait four to six months between injections. Once cortisone's effectiveness has worn off, surgery is usually considered, if it is at all practical.

Systemic corticosteroids: When multiple joints are involved, injections are not practical and systemic corticosteroid must be used. Patients taking corticosteroids by mouth should be cautioned not to just stop taking them; their use must be decreased gradually, following the physician's instructions. Abrupt withdrawal can cause problems with the body's natural hormone production and can result in death.

Side effects of corticosteroids include gastrointestinal problems, hypertension, congestive heart failure, diabetes, bleeding, osteoporosis, and muscle wasting. Corticosteroid use can also affect appearance, with upsetting results to the arthritis victims. Fluid retention, increased appetite, weight gain, redistribution of body fat, rounding of the face, fatty tissue on the trunk and a fat pad at the base of the neck can all occur. A low-salt, low-calorie diet is often recommended. Corticosteroids may be taken with other drugs, but patients should check with their doctors first.

30

DRUGS USED TO TREAT GOUT

This Key covers the drugs used in the treatment of gout, beginning with Colchicine™ and including medications to lower uric acid levels.

Colchicine™: As mentioned in Key 8, the most specific drug for eliminating a gouty attack is Colchicine™, which has been around since the time of Hippocrates. When an acute attack hits, it is taken hourly until pain becomes tolerable or side effects develop. It is important to begin the medicine within the first two days of the attack. (If the joint does not improve on Colchicine™, the condition is not gout.) According to the Arthritis Foundation, to prevent further attacks you may need to take the drug for six months or longer.

Side effects of taking Colchicine™ by mouth include diarrhea, nausea, and abdominal cramps. However, the drug can be given by injection to sidestep these problems.

Uricosuric drugs: Uricosuric drugs lower uric acid levels. However, they are not quick acting antidotes for acute attacks but take several months to be effective. They work by blocking absorption of uric acid by the kidneys so that it is passed in urine. Uricosuric drugs help to eliminate painful tophi and to prevent further attacks of gout. Common uricosurics include probenicid (Benemid™, Parbenem™, and Probalan™) and sulfinpyrazone (Anturane™). Ironically, these drugs can actually bring on an acute attack of gout when they are first taken. To avoid this, your doctor may advise you to take Colchicine™ or anti-inflammatory drugs for several months when you first start taking uricosuric drugs.

Uricosuric drugs must be taken continually or uric acid levels will rise again. In addition, large amounts of fluids must be taken to dilute the urine and prevent uric acid levels from building up and causing painful kidney stones.

Side effects of these drugs include nausea, skin rash, stomach upset, and headaches. Patients taking them should drink lots of fluids and avoid aspirin.

Drugs that block production of uric acid: Allopurinol (Lopurin™, Zurinol™, Zyloprim™) is a drug that reduces the production of uric acid by the body, rather than blocking its absorption by the kidneys. It is the best gout medication for anyone with kidney problems. Like uricosuric drugs, these medications must be taken continually or uric acid levels will rise again.

Side effects of these drugs include skin rash and stomach upset. Like uricosuric drugs, these medications can cause an acute attack of gout when they are first taken. To avoid this, your doctor may advise you to take Colchicine™ or anti-inflammatory drugs for several months when you first start taking allopurinol.

Sodium bicarbonate: Regular doses of sodium bicarbonate can help to neutralize uric acid.

31

OTHER DRUGS USED IN THE TREATMENT OF ARTHRITIS

This Key covers a variety of drugs that are used less commonly to treat arthritis-related symptoms than those described in the previous keys.

Antibiotics: As mentioned in Key 10, some forms of arthritis are caused by the body's response to a bacterial infection such as that occurring with Lyme disease or gonorrhea. In these cases, treatment with an antibiotic such as penicillin can relieve symptoms by alleviating the cause. However, antibiotics must be taken soon after the initial infection sets in, to be most effective.[19]

Antidepressants: Depression can be an unwelcome companion to arthritis. However, older persons should use caution when taking antidepressants such as Elavil™. For example, the effective dosage for these drugs is lower at older ages than at younger ages. Moreover, according to Dr. Stephen Wegener of the University of Virginia Medical Center, their use can be particularly traumatic for older adults.[20] Side effects include drowsiness, sedation, insomnia, confusion, cardiovascular problems, gastrointestinal problems, congestion, dry eyes, and genitourinary problems. In order to cut down on drowsiness, it may be useful to take the entire dose before bedtime.

---

[19]Dominick Bosco and Gloria McVeigh, *Prevention,* February, 1991, p. 68.
[20]Stephen T. Wegener, "Psychological and Behavioral Aspects of Chronic Arthritis," *A Guide to Arthritis Home Health Care,* 1988, p. 221.

Antimalarials used to treat lupus: Although there is no known connection between lupus and malaria, antimalarial drugs, particularly hydroxychloroquine (Plaquenil™), are sometimes prescribed for lupus patients. (Plaquenil™ is also sometimes prescribed for rheumatoid arthritis.) These drugs may allow lupus sufferers to avoid taking steroids and can be effective against fever, joint pains, and inflammation of the lining of the lungs. Because antimalarials can affect the eyes, regular monitoring by an eye doctor is important for patients taking the drug. Plaquenil™ can also cause a skin rash, nausea, vomiting, diarrhea, muscle weakness, nervousness, headache, and dizziness.

DMSO: DMSO (dimethyl sulfoxide) is a drug used by veterinarians and is also sold as an industrial solvent. It has not been approved by the Food and Drug Administration and is available only illegally for medical use for humans.

Every so often there is a flurry of attention about DMSO in which proponents claim that it works miracles against arthritis, cancer, and other ailments and that its availability is being suppressed by the government. However, there is no scientific evidence that DMSO is beneficial for arthritis other than as a pain reliever similar to aspirin.[21] It is a potentially dangerous drug, because those who take it may waste precious time when they could be taking other measures that would actually help their condition.

DMSO is usually available only in strengths suitable for animals other than humans. It can cause nausea, headaches, and skin rashes. Other side effects include a garlic taste in the mouth, skin rashes, headache, nausea, and diarrhea. DMSO also can cause night blindness, blurred vision, and cataracts.

---

[21]Arthritis Foundation, *Arthritis Fact Book*, 1986, p. 23.

Drugs available from Mexican clinics. A word of caution: Mexican clinics offering mysterious medicines that are touted as "miracles drugs" have sprung up near the United States border. These medications are illegal in the United States for a good reason—they can be poisonous and sometimes lead to death.

Experimental drugs. Rheumatologists continue to experiment with medications and combinations of medications. Some of the drugs presently being tried are cyclosporine, interferon, amiprilose hydrochloride, omega-3 fatty acids, and monoclonal antibodies. New experimental drugs include interleukin-2, butoxamine, and ICI-18.

Etridonate cyclical therapy: This new treatment, which is currently used in Paget's disease, has received wide publicity as the hope for postmenopausal women who develop osteoporosis. In etridonate cyclical therapy (ECT), the individual first takes a drug called etridonate disodium, followed by calcium. The first slows down bone resorption, and the second aids proper bone formation. The treatment has proved highly successful in two studies, one in Denmark and one in the United States. In the U.S. study at Emory University in Atlanta, women who received ECT had 50 percent fewer fractures than women who received a placebo. There was also an average increase of 5 percent of bone mass after two years of treatment. The drug can be administered orally and has no negative side effects. However, further research is needed.

H2 antagonists: These drugs can protect against the gastrointestinal problems caused by NSAIDS by reducing the amount of acid in the stomach. H2 antagonists include Tagamet™, Zantac™, and famotidine.

Misoprostol: This drug, also known by its trade name, Cytotec™, is a welcome preventative for the stomach ulcers that can result from anti-inflammatory drugs. It works by replacing some of the prostaglandins that are destroyed by taking NSAIDS. Side effects may include diarrhea and cramping in the beginning of treatment, but this often clears up. At this writing, misoprostol is the only drug approved to prevent stomach ulcers caused by NSAIDS. The drug is not used for treatment of ulcers.

Photopheresis: Photopheresis destroys abnormal, immune system cells (T cells) by removing blood from the body mechanically, treating it with ultraviolet light, and then returning it to the body. At this writing, this procedure is approved only for treatment of T-cell lymphoma, but the Food and Drug Administration is presently considering approval of its use for scleroderma.

Sucralfate: This drug coats the stomach and duodenum to prevent gastrointestinal problems caused by NSAIDS. Side effects include constipation or diarrhea, and the drug may affect the absorption of other drugs.

32

EXERCISE

Hippocrates, living five centuries before Christ, was one of the first to understand the value of exercise in hindering the march of time. He said, "All parts of the body which have a function, if used in moderation and exercised in labors to which each is accustomed, become thereby well-developed and age slowly; but if unused and left idle, they become liable to disease, defective in growth, and age quickly."

If your response to exercise is, "I'm too old to start now," think twice. Exercise—started at any age, even after a long period of inactivity—has benefits. Maximum oxygen consumption (VO2 max) is an example. The greater a person's VO2, the greater his or her endurance. Studies have shown that, even for older people who have been inactive previously, an aerobic exercise program results in an average increase in VO2 max of 10 to 30 percent.

On top of improved overall fitness, regular exercise benefits arthritis sufferers in a number of other ways including:
- building and maintaining muscle strength.
- reducing fatigue.
- supporting the joints through stronger muscles and ligaments.
- supporting mobility.
- reducing stress on joints through stronger supportive tissue.
- nourishing the joint through increasing the supply of synovial fluid.
- preventing joint deformities.

- improving joint deformities.

Aerobic exercise. There are four major types of exercise—aerobic, range-of-motion, stretching, and strengthening. The latter three are covered in Key 21. This Key covers the benefits of aerobic exercise and provides information about the Arthritis Foundation's exercise programs.

Aerobic exercise, which improves overall fitness, includes walking, stationary bicycling, swimming, and low-impact aerobics. In order for exercise to be aerobic, your pulse must be within the target heart rate for your age (the target zone is 60 to 75 percent of your maximum workout rate during vigorous exercise). The following will help you figure out your maximum rate:

- To take your pulse, press your index (second) finger and third finger of one hand firmly against the wrist just below the thumb side of the other hand.
- Count the beats for fifteen seconds, then multiply by four.
- To figure your maximum rate, subtract your age from the number 220.
- When exercising, your heart should not beat more times per minute than this number; it should be in the range of 60 to 75 percent of the maximum workout rate.

For example, if you are age 50 your maximum workout rate is 170 beats per minute and the range that you should be in is 102 to 143 beats per minute. Your target zone should never go below 100 beats per minute.

For aerobic fitness, your pulse should reach this rate for 20 to 30 minutes at least three times a week. However, you should work up to this amount of exercise in five-minute increments. The exercise program should include a warm-up, conditioning exercise, and a cooldown.

Most experts recommend that every aerobic session

have a warm-up and cool-down period of three to five minutes. The intensity of these periods should be half-way between the previous activity and the aerobic activity. Slow walking, light calisthenics, and stretching are warm-up activities.

Walking. Walking is highly recommended to prevent osteoporosis, is one of the most readily available exercises for people of all ages, and has the distinct advantage of being free. For most older people, walking results in a target heart zone that is intense enough to be aerobic if performed for a long enough time. For many older people, walking for half an hour to an hour three times a week is aerobic. Follow these tips from the Public Health Service's Health Older People Program to get started on a regular regimen.

- Wear comfortable shoes with good arch supports. They should be made of materials that breathe, like leather or nylon.
- Take long strides at a steady pace. Keep your head erect, back straight, and stomach flat. Point your toes straight ahead, and let your arms swing loosely at your sides.
- Start a regular routine by walking every other day for about 15 minutes. Warm up by walking slowly for about five minutes, then faster for five minutes. Then cool down by walking slowly for the last five.
- Listen to your body. Brisk walking should make your heart beat faster and your breathing deeper. Stop if you find yourself panting, feeling nauseous, or unable to get your breathing back to normal within ten minutes.
- Gradually increase your distance and the length of your stride. In five weeks, you should be walking about a mile and be ready to increase the frequency of your walking to five times a week. Continue five

minutes of slow walking at the beginning and the end, but extend your brisk walking period.

- Add a time and distance goal to your walking sessions. After seven weeks, try walking a mile in 20 minutes. Next, increase your distance and stick to the 20-minute goal. A good goal to work up to (over about 15 weeks) is walking three miles in 45 minutes.
- Remember good walking form. Land on the heel of your foot and move forward to spring off the ball. You'll tire or become sore more quickly by walking only on the ball of your feet or if you are flat-footed.

Preparing for exercise: Before you start an exercise program, you should see a doctor or physical therapist and discuss the types of exercise to avoid in order to protect your joints. Generally, however, it is advisable to stay away from exercise that jars the joints such as jogging and high-impact aerobics. You might also want to avoid anything that might injure arthritic joints such as contact sports.

When pain and stiffness are a problem, preparing for exercise by massaging the joint, or applying heat or cold may help. For information on using heat and cold, see Key 34.

Exercise programs sponsored by the Arthritis Foundation: Arthritis Foundation chapters offer two exercise programs that you may want to take advantage of. The first program, PACE, stands for "People With Arthritis Can Exercise." It includes exercises designed specifically for people with arthritis. Two levels of the program are available—basic and advanced. The first level is for people with significant problems and includes people who are in wheelchairs. The second level is for people with mild joint problems who tire easily. The program uses gentle exercise to increase joint flexibility, range-of-motion, muscle strength, and overall stamina.

The classes are conducted by an instructor who has undergone a special Arthritis Foundation training. Any adult who can walk independently, possibly with assistive devices, can participate. You must be able to sit up in a straight-back chair. The program is available on videotape. For information, call (800) PACE-236; in Virginia call collect (703) 391-7896.

The second program, the Arthritis Aquatics Program, offers recreational exercises in a heated pool. Participants can actually do more in water with less pain than they can out of it because of the buoyancy of the water. The benefits are stronger joints that are less stiff.

33

DIET

Most leading rheumatologists assert emphatically that no food or special diet can cause or cure arthritis. In other words, there is no such thing as an arthritis diet.

At the same time, however, if you have arthritis, you should pay attention to several nutritional considerations, including the relationship of foods rich in purines to gout, the relationship between obesity and arthritis, the effects of medicines on diet, the need for calcium and vitamin D to prevent bone loss, the effect of aging on nutritional needs, and the need for a well-balanced diet. The following presents basic information about these factors.

Gout: This is the only arthritic disease that can be helped by avoiding certain foods. If you have gout you should stay away from alcohol, brains, liver, sweetbreads, and kidneys.

Obesity: The fact that obesity is almost synonymous with specific forms of arthritis has been discussed throughout this book. Extra weight puts extra stress on weight-bearing joints. In addition, overweight people tend to be less active than thinner people, which can lead to stiffening of the joints.

Vitamin D and calcium: Including calcium in the daily diet is one way to guard against osteoporosis. Foods rich in calcium include milk, yogurt, cheese, and other dairy products; dark green leafy vegetables; and salmon. As mentioned in Key 15, both older men and women should take in 1,200 to 1,500 milligrams of calcium a day.

The "sun" vitamin, vitamin D, is also one of the keys to preventing osteoporosis. Older people often have to take special measures to be sure that they get adequate amounts of the vitamin because their skin's ability to produce it decreases over time. Vitamin D can be found in sunshine and milk. However, Dr. Grayzel points out that too much vitamin D can cause as many problems as too little. If you do not eat or drink many dairy products or get much sun, ask your doctor's advice on whether you should take a vitamin D supplement.

The effect of medicines on diet: If you are taking any medication, you should check with your doctor to see how it may affect your nutrition. For example, many diuretics rob the body of potassium, corticosteroids often cause weight gain and redistribution, and aspirin causes excretion of vitamin C in urine. On the other hand, some medications contain too much of certain nutrients such as sodium, which can lead to hypertension, heart disease, and other conditions. Antacids and steroids, for example, are high in sodium.

Basics of nutrition and aging: As people age, the body's basic need for nutrients such as proteins, carbohydrates, vitamins, and minerals remains unchanged. However, the body's need for calories decreases due to physical changes and decreasing activity. The result is that many people put on weight as they age.

The National Institute on Aging (NIA), part of the National Institutes on Health, recommends that older adults limit their intake of fatty foods, sweets, salty snack foods, high-calorie drinks, and alcohol. These foods are high in calories but not nutrients. NIA points out that a nutritious diet provides minerals, vitamins, and calories from proteins, carbohydrates, and some fats. Such a diet must include a variety of foods from all the major food groups: fruits and vegetables; whole grain and enriched breads, cereals, and grain products such as rice and pasta; fish, poultry, meats, eggs, and dry beans and peas; and milk, cheese, and other dairy products.

Limiting the amount of fat in the diet may help prevent weight gain, which is an important factor in controlling arthritis. Limiting fat may also help protect against heart disease and certain types of cancer. NIA also recommends reducing salt intake.

The following is a list of the major nutrients that you should include in your diet:

- *Protein.* Protein is the basic material in all body cells. It also is required for growth and repair of body cells and helps the body resist disease. During digestion, food proteins are broken down into simple nutrients called amino acids, which are the building blocks of life. The body then reassembles these into the types of proteins it needs.

  Many foods contain protein. The proteins in meats, fish, dairy products, and eggs contain the essential amino acids in proper amounts for adults. These are complete proteins. The easiest way to get complete amino acids is to eat some of these foods every day. Plant foods such as dry peas and beans, grains, nuts, and seeds contain "incomplete" proteins, so called because not all the essential amino acids are present. However, when one of these foods is combined with an animal protein (milk and cereal, for example) or when certain plant proteins are combined (such as rice with beans), they form complete proteins. Foods high in protein also provide essential vitamins and minerals.

- *Carbohydrates.* There are two types of carbohydrates. "Complex" carbohydrates are starches present in grains, cereals, legumes, potatoes, and other vegetables, and sugars present in fruits and milk. These foods are good sources of vitamins, minerals, fiber, and calories. "Simple" sugars are found in desserts, candy, honey, syrup, and other sugary foods. These are the foods that we love to eat but have to limit since they provide few nutrients.

Bread and cereals are more nutritious if made from whole grains. Examples are whole wheat and rye breads and crackers, whole wheat cereals, bran, oatmeal, barley, brown rice, and cornmeal.

- *Fats.* Fats are concentrated sources of calories. Some fat is needed in the diet because it provides essential amino acids and gives flavor to food. However, the typical American diet is too high in fat and cholesterol. Low-fat foods include fish, poultry, lean meats, dry beans and peas, skim milk, yogurt, buttermilk, fruits, vegetables, and grains. Eggs and organ meats should be limited, as well as butter, cream, mayonnaise, margarine, oils, lard, certain prepared foods (for example, fast-food hamburgers), and snack foods such as potato chips.
- *Vitamins and minerals.* These are needed by the body in relatively small amounts. The fat-soluble vitamins A, D, E, and K are absorbed along with fat from various foods and are stored in the body. The water-soluble vitamins, the Bs and C, generally are not stored. Minerals such as calcium, phosphorus, iron, iodine, magnesium, and zinc are also required for building body tissues and regulating their functions.

Vitamins and minerals are abundant in fruit, vegetables, meats, dairy products, and whole grain or enriched breads and cereals.

As mentioned above, older adults should pay attention to their need for calcium and vitamin D.

Fiber: Another important part of the diet is fiber. The definitive role of fiber is not known, but it can help prevent constipation, intestinal disorders, and cancer of the colon.

The best way to include fiber in the diet is to eat whole grain breads and cereals and plenty of vegetables and fruits. Adding a few tablespoons of unprocessed bran, which is high in fiber, to cereal and other foods is acceptable. However, an excessive intake of bran can decrease the body's absorption of minerals such as iron and calcium.

34

HOT AND COLD TREATMENTS

Application of hot and cold, also known as thermotherapy and cyrotherapy, respectively, can provide welcome relief for pain.

Heat: Heat is one of the oldest techniques for relieving pain. It works by increasing the flow of blood to the affected area and changing the perception of pain. There are a myriad of ways to apply heat to your body; in most cases, methods of applying heat should *not* be combined.

There are two types of thermotherapy: surface and deep heat. Surface heat, such as heating pads and paraffin, does not penetrate below the skin. Deep heat, in contrast, warms up the joint. It is applied by a physical therapist with sophisticated shortwave or microwave equipment. Rheumatologists suggest caution about using deep heat directly over a joint as it can exacerbate the problem, however.

When using either heat or cold, it is important to guard against burning or frostbite by keeping the source of heat or cold next to the skin for no longer than 20 minutes. It is often advisable to keep moving the source so that it isn't against one spot too long.

Here's information on some of the gadgets and techniques available for applying heat.

- *Electric or battery-powered heating garments.* These include battery-operated warming mittens and socks and electrically heated cuffs for warming hands.

- *Heat lamps*. These use infrared current to provide penetrating heat for muscles. Heat lamps are available in lightweight and portable models. Be sure to check with a physician before using this treatment, since individuals with certain conditions such as heart disease should not use infrared heat.

- *Heating pads*. These are available in both dry and dry/moist heat. They provide limited help for specific painful parts of the body.

- *Hot tubs and whirlpools*. These popular treatments combine the relaxing comfort of a warm pool or bathtub with a water jet that is like a shower massager. Generally, there is little difference between the two, except that a hot tub holds two or more people and a whirlpool can be the size of a small foot bath. You can also use a whirlpool attachment that fits in your bathtub.

- *Hot packs*. These are cloth pouches filled with silicate gel that are heated and applied to afflicted areas over several layers of towels to protect the skin.

- *Hot-water bottles*. While hot water bottles are affordable, they can be hard for some people to use. Like heating pads, they provide help only for limited parts of the body. If they work for you, you may want more than one to apply to multiple joints.

- *Knee or elbow warmers*. These are tubular pieces of wool or acrylic that provide warmth and protection to joints.

- *Microwave heat*. Heat applied through microwave achieves deep heat without overheating the skin. It is simpler to use than other deep heat equipment like shortwave diathermy and is comfortable for the arthritis sufferer to use.

- *Saunas and steamrooms*. Both saunas and steamrooms are very hot rooms; the first is extremely dry, and the second is extremely humid.

- *Shortwave heat.* Heat applied by shortwave is less effective than formerly thought. You might want to avoid this one.
- *Thermoelastic products.* Made from wool and elastic fibers, these products are wonderfully warm and are available for hands, knees, and elbows.
- *Ultrasound heat.* Deep heat applied through ultrasound can help relieve the symptoms of bursitis and tendonitis.
- *Warm and hot baths.* Dava Sobel and Arthur C. Klein reported that half of the participants in their national study of 1,051 individuals with arthritis take a daily warm or hot bath for pain relief.[22] Sobel and Klein, authors of *Backache Relief* and *Arthritis: What Works,* found that many survey participants also feel a warm or hot bath relieves stiffness. For those who do not like baths, warm or hot showers are equally effective.
- *Wax.* A paraffin bath uses moist heat to treat pain. The wax can be heated in a double boiler or a commerical thermostatically controlled paraffin bath unit. The wax should be melted to 49°C or 120°F.[23] It should never go over 54.4°C or 130°F.

  When paraffin is used on the hand, it can be dipped directly into the melted wax. Other parts of the body require painting or wrapping. Be sure there are no open wounds on the area being exposed to wax and that you are not allegeric to paraffin.
- *Wet towels.* This is an economical way of applying heat to limited parts of the body such as the shoulders. The towel may be heated in a microwave.

---

[22]Dava Sobel and Arthur C. Klein, *Arthritis: What Works,* St. Martin's Press, 1989, p. 331.
[23] Mathew H. M. Lee and Masayoshi Itoh, "Rehabilitation," *The Merck Manual of Geriatrics*, 1990, p. 255.

Cold: Cold can reduce muscle spasms, appears to decrease cartilage damage, and stimulates the production of pain-relieving endorphins. However, you should be careful not to apply too much cold as it can cause stiffness.

An ice-pack, gel-type pack, plastic baggie with ice in it, or bag of frozen vegetables can all be used against a painful area to relieve discomfort. Ice should never be placed directly on the skin.

Heat and cold: Some people find that alternating heat and cold is most effective. For example, you might alternate a hot pack with an ice pack.

Contrast baths: Combined warm and cold water soaks can help relieve stiffness. One option is to alternate hot and cold soaks for a half hour, never spending longer than a minute in the cool water. Check with a physical therapist first to determine the correct water temperature and the amount of time to spend in each bath.

35

REST AND RELAXATION

In balance with exercise, rest and relaxation are an important part of arthritis treatment. The pain of arthritis often involves tight muscles and other related physical symptoms, as well as anxiety. In fact, studies have shown that relaxation can lessen the perception of pain among people with arthritis.[24] Most physicians advise patients to rest when symptoms are increasing and get more exercise when they are subsiding. There are a number of techniques for relaxation, some of which are listed below.

- *Deep breathing*. This is a technique for averting shallow, ineffective breathing by learning to breathe deeply and slowly. It is part of many other relaxation techniques.
- *Autogenic relaxing*. This technique has the advantage of not being stressful to joints. You talk yourself into relaxing. Get comfortable and progressively tell different parts of your body to relax: "My toes are now relaxed. The balls of my feet are now relaxed."
- *Biofeedback*. With this technique, you relax by receiving "feedback" from specific body responses that can tell you when you are relaxed and when you are tense. During biofeedback you are hooked up to electric equipment that monitors these physical reactions and gives you information on them. (You will not be shocked by the electricity.) This technique is very

---

[24] Stephen T. Wegener and Cynthia Stabenow Kulp, "The Management of Arthritis Pain," *A Guide to Arthritis Home Health Care*, 1988, p. 165.

useful for people who have a hard time knowing when their body is relaxed.

- *Focusing.* Based on research at the University of Chicago, this technigue, which is becoming so popular that some nursing schools are teaching it, involves learning to identify the way personal problems manifest themselves in the body. In focusing, you make contact with an internal bodily awareness through six specific movements. The technique is taught in a book called, appropriately, *Focusing,* written by Eugene T. Gwendlin, Ph. D., and published by Everest House or Bantam Books.

- *Imagery/creative visualization.* This technique uses mental imagery to improve health and attitudes and to block pain perception. The individual visualizes a favorite place that is associated with peaceful feelings or makes one up, such as floating on a cloud. The classic book that shows how to use imagery is *Creative Visualization* by Shakti Gawain, published by New Age Bantam Books.

- *Meditation.* This technique involves concentrating on one sound or thought in order to reach a relaxed, peaceful state. When done properly, meditation helps slow down your breathing, and other physical signs of relaxation will be present. Meditation tapes are available in most bookstores.

- *Prayer.* For many, prayer is a way of relaxing and reaching a peaceful state of mind.

- *Self-hypnosis.* Self-hypnosis is a technique for clearing your mind of all extraneous thoughts so that you can concentrate on relaxing. It can help you sleep better and release tension.

36

SLEEP

When arthritis strikes, the result can be fatigue. Persons with arthritis are more likely to have sleep disturbances than others the same age.[25]

Normal sleep has two important cycles—rapid eye movement sleep (REM) and non-REM sleep. All of us have four or five of both of these cycles per night. With aging, the amount of time spent in REM sleep decreases, which may be the reason older people are considered "light sleepers."

At any age you need to get from seven to eight hours of sleep a night. However, the pattern for how you achieve those hours changes with age. Younger people tend to get their sleep all at one time; when people are older, sleep is broken up.

Sleep disorders: Insomnia is disturbing at any age. It is the most common sleep problem and is usually a symptom of another problem, rather than being the problem in and of itself. Insomnia means taking a long time to fall asleep (more than half an hour or 45 minutes), waking up many times each night, or waking up early and not being able to get back to sleep.

Sleep apnea is a problem in which sleeping stops for up to two minutes and the person struggles to breath, while remaining unaware of what is happening. Two clues to the existence of this condition are daytime sleepiness and loud snoring. Gadgets are available to

---

[25]Stephen T. Wegener and Cynthia Stabenow Kulp, "Fatigue and Sleep Disturbance in Arthritis," *A Guide to Arthritis Home Health Care*, 1988, p. 192.

help people with this problem, including devices to keep people off their backs.

Nocturnal myoclonus is characterized by leg twitches that cause you to wake. The cause is not known.

If you have any of these symptoms you should discuss them with your doctor.

Tips for getting a good night's sleep: These tips, which are adapted from suggestions made by the National Institute on Aging, will help you get a good night's sleep.

- Follow a regular schedule—go to sleep and get up at the same time each day.
- Try to exercise at regular times each day. Moderate physical activity two to four hours before bedtime may improve your sleep.
- To adjust your internal sleep clock, try to get some exposure to the natural light in the afternoon each day.
- Be aware of what you eat. Avoid drinking caffeinated beverages (coffee, tea, soft drinks such as cola, chocolate) late in the day. Caffeine is a stimulant, and can keep you awake. Monosodium glutamate (MSG), a seasoning used in some Chinese cooking, can have the same effect. If you like a snack before bed, a glass of warm milk may help.
- Don't drink alcohol or smoke cigarettes to help you sleep. Drinking even small amounts of alcohol can make it harder to stay asleep. Nicotine in cigarettes is a stimulant.
- Develop a bedtime routine. Do the same things each night to tell your body that it's time to run down. Some people watch the evening news, read a book, or soak in a warm tub.
- Try taking a warm bath before getting into bed.
- Use your bedroom only for sleeping. After turning off the light, give yourself about fifteen minutes of

trying to fall asleep. If you are still awake or if you lose your drowsiness, get up and go into another room until you feel sleepy again.

- Be sure to take your medication at the right times to cut down on pain during the night.
- Try using aids such as specially shaped pillows or footboards to maintain good posture while sleeping.
- Try out some of the relaxation techniques discussed in the previous key.
- Try to do restful, peaceful things before you go to sleep; don't try to work out problems while you are trying to nod off.

In addition, a comfortable bed with a good comfortable, firm mattress is important. The bed should support the spine and not sag in the middle. You may want to consider a heated waterbed—but try it before you buy it. They are expensive, and although some people swear by them, others can't stand them. An electric blanket or mattress pad may also be helpful. In order to avoid flexion contractures, the best position for sleep is flat on the back with the muscles extended as much as possible.

When to see a doctor: If you are so tired during the day that you can not function normally and the problem lasts for two or three weeks, you should contact your family doctor or a sleep disorder specialist.

Sleeping positions for specific problems: Depending on which joints are involved, you may want to try different positions to relieve pain. Use caution, however, and discuss sleeping positions with a doctor or physical therapist; sleeping with a pillow under the knees, for example, can cause knee contractures (locking).

37

PAIN MANAGEMENT

Pain is the body's straightforward way of telling you that something has gone awry. It gets your attention. Pain is the provoking symptom that sends its victims in search of relief. For individuals with arthritis, pain is complex. It can be acute, chronic, or both; it can be jabbing, crushing, or a dull ache. It can cause you to "take to bed" permanently or just keep you off the tennis court while you continue to jog. And it can come and go, providing welcome periods of relief.

Pain is impossible to measure. There is no blood test, gauge, or litmus test to quantify it. Only the sufferer can describe it. And the description is necessarily subjective; the pain that may be piercing to you may be but a twinge to another. Types may include:

Acute pain: This is the most common type of pain and the most treatable with such measures as analgesic drugs, rest, and restrictions on activity. Usually the arthritis sufferer with acute pain can return to painless and full functioning. Acute pain is characteristic of such conditions as gout or bursitis.

Chronic pain: Chronic pain is long-term, and the cause is often elusive. By definition, chronic pain lasts more than six months. It is usually a lifelong companion, frequently disrupting your whole life. It is harder to treat than acute pain, partly because the long-term use of strong drugs such as steroids is discouraged. Examples include low back pain and recurrent headaches.

Intermittent pain: Intermittent pain is chronic pain that comes and goes. While the pain is always there in some form, its strength varies. Usually activities have to be planned around periods of pain remission. Intermittent pain is common in many forms of arthritis.

There are a number of measures to control or ease pain, many of which are discussed throughout this book. Medications are covered in Keys 24–31. In addition, tips on how to dress and get around with a minimal amount of pain can be found in Key 44. The following pain treatments are not mentioned elsewhere in the book.

Acupuncture: In acupunture, a series of very thin needles is inserted at specific points on the body remote from the area of pain. The needle is either twirled in place, or a low voltage electric current is applied. It is not known how acupuncture works, but one theory suggests that it increases "feel good" hormones called endorphins which are thought to be painkillers.

Cognitive interventions: Authors Stephen T. Wegener and Cynthia Stabenow Kulp describe three cognitive strategies that research indicates may be useful in modifying the pain people experience.[26] The techniques are attention diversion, refocusing, and pain-inoculation training.

Attention diversion means reducing the impact of pain by focusing on other things. For example, you might visualize and describe, out loud or to yourself, a favorite vacation spot—the colors, the smells, the tastes. Using every possible sense enhances the process. The goal is to focus attention away from pain and to become distracted by something absorbing and pleasant.

Refocusing is often used spontaneously to distract from pain. It may include reading, watching a sport, or changing the way you think about pain. For example, you may think of pangs and twinges not as pain, but as your body's message to you to slow down. Or you might

---

[26]Stephen T. Wegener and Cynthia Stabenow Kulp, *A Guide to Arthritis Home Health Care*, 1988, pp. 170–74.

focus on what you can do and not what you can't do.

Pain inoculation training involves preparing for the pain mentally first so that when it comes you are prepared for it. It helps you develop a plan for managing your pain.

Liniments. While there is no scientific evidence that liniments provide pain relief, many people believe that they get help from stimulating the affected area with products such as Ben-Gay™, Aspercreme™, Tiger Balm™, and Absorbine Junior™.

Massage: Massage is relaxing and can help reduce stiffness and pain by increasing blood flow to the massaged area and warming it. Two theories to explain massage's effectiveness are that it relieves pain by releasing hormones that make people feel good and it stimulates nerves that block the body's pain pathways.

Dr. Fred G, Krantowitz, author of *Taking Control of Arthritis,* prefers that a physical therapist or similar health care professional administer massages to assure that the person is familiar with handling medical problems.[27] For example, he points out, inflamed joints should never be massaged directly.

Your nurse or physical therapist can show you how to massage yourself, using powder or baby oil to make it easier. For example, the therapist may show you how to try a deep, circular movement on your sore back or a kneading motion on your stiff neck.

Pain clinics: Pain clinics, staffed solely by health professionals who specialize in helping people cope with pain, are growing in popularity. Some pain clinics are free-standing, while others are parts of larger institutions. For people with chronic pain, they can be extremely helpful.

Positioning: Often arthritis sufferers carefully position pillows in strategic places to relieve pain. While it

---

[27]Fred G. Krantowitz, *Taking Control of Arthritis,* Harper Collins, 1990, p. 119.

may be effective for relieving pain, such positioning can cause knees and elbows to "lock" in position, causing flexion contractures. Joints should be extended when resting; splints may be useful. (Key 39).

TENS: TENS, a popular treatment for chronic pain, stands for transcutaneous electrical nerve stimulation. Dating back in theory to the days when electric eels were used to ease pain, TENS delivers low-frequency electric current from a small battery pack through electrodes placed on the skin.

The TENS user feels a mild tingling sensation. The effect of TENS varies tremendously; some people swear by it, while others can't figure out what all the excitement is about. For some, it works on one problem and not another.

For those who find TENS effective, it may be used on a long-term basis or temporarily during painful episodes. It may be applied several times a day for up to a couple of hours. TENS is safe to use over a long period of time but should not be used by anyone with a pacemaker or dysrhythmia. A prescription is required and a home unit costs at least two hundred dollars. Some insurance policies cover the cost.

Traction: Traction relieves pain by pulling apart constricted joint spaces and relieving pinched nerves. Certain forms, such as spinal traction, force the spine to rest by immobolizing the patient. There are a number of ways traction may be utilized—by machine or by using weights and pulleys, for example. Traction may be applied intermittently or continuously.

Traction should *never* be tried without the advice and assistance of a physical therapist; if it is done improperly, serious damage may result.

38

JOINT PROTECTION

Protecting joints is a fundamental part of arthritis treatment. In fact, not protecting joints is a bit like applying salt to an open wound—it painfully aggravates an already existing problem.

Protecting joints means carrying out all activities in the best way possible to reduce stress. There are many joint protecting devices available; these are described in the next Key. But first, you need to understand and follow basic joint protecting principles as you carry out your everyday activities.

- Pay attention to pain. "Toughing it out" and continuing to apply pressure to a painful joint can result in permanent damage.

- Conserve energy so you approach the most difficult tasks when you are strongest. Don't try to do too much at one time.

- Try to use larger joints when you can, not small joints. In other words, shove a door open with your shoulder instead of your hand, open a jar with a wrist action rather than using only your fingers.

- Use your stronger joints, and protect weaker ones. For example, when climbing, use your stronger leg going up and your weaker one going down.

- Use two hands instead of one.

- Try not to let joints remain in one position too long.

- Extend your joints as far as possible as often as you can. Extending joints keeps them mobile.

- Control your weight. Extra pounds puts stress on weight-bearing joints such as the hips, the knees, the back, and the feet.

- Use health aids and assistive and labor-saving devices, long-handled reachers, and Velcro™ closures, all of which help keep stress off problem joints.
- Good posture protects joints. Have a physical therapist check your posture in all positions—standing, walking, sitting, lying in bed—to make sure that your posture is not hurting your joints.
- Working at appropriate heights not only protects joints, but also helps to conserve energy. According to the Arthritis Foundation: "Joints are protected because they are used in the position of least stress. Energy is conserved because the body is positioned in a place requiring the least amount of energy to complete a task."[28]

[28]Arthritis Foundation, *Self-Care for Osteoarthritis and Rheumatoid Arthritis,* 1983, p. 18.

39

SPLINTS AND OTHER PROTECTIVE DEVICES

Splints provide rest and protection for joints when arthritis symptoms are flaring. They may also stabilize a joint and keep it from deformity. Different splints and other protective devices are available for the various joints in the body, ranging from elastic supports to shoe lifts. Here are some of those most commonly used for arthritis:

- *Cervical collar.* This device immobilizes the neck, relieving pain and protecting it from "locking" in position.

- *Corset.* Corsets provide stability for the thoracic or lumbar spine. However, prolonged use can cause weakening of muscles.

- *Leg braces.* Types of leg braces available include those for disability of the ankle, knee, and hip. Braces should be chosen carefully; some are not practical for older adults because of their weight.

- *Orthopedic shoes.* These are available commercially or may be custom made. They may be designed to wear with shoe inserts (see below). Orthopedic shoes can help you improve your walking and can redistribute weight to be kinder on painful joints. Examples are shoes with Thomas heels to prevent the feet from rolling forward, metatarsal bars to relieve pressure on the ball of the foot, or wedges to prevent inward turning of the heel.

- *Shoe inserts.* These redistribute weight to unafflicted areas of the feet.

- *Splints.* Splints are used to help rest joints, to reduce stress on joints, and to prevent deformity. Your physician may prescribe one of the numerous splints available to stabilize and immobilize a joint. The support they provide can actually prevent crippling. Examples of splints for the hand are functional wrist splints, resting hand splints, PIP extension splints, finger ring splints, and thumb splints.

- *Walking aids.* These can help you get around after surgery, during a flare-up, or if you have a chronic disability. Walkers provide stability for the user but are cumbersome for getting around, do not bear weight as well as other options, and cannot be used going up and down stairs. Ordinary crutches are not used very often by older adults because they require significant upper body strength. However, one type of crutch, called a Canadian crutch, has arm supports and hand grips, making it more appropriate for older people. Canes help maintain balance and reduce the amount of weight placed on the hip.
- *Wheelchair.* Wheelchairs come in indoor and outdoor models and may be self-propelling or motorized. The American Association of Retired Persons offers a guide to purchasing wheelchairs that describes the different types and models and available accessories. The guide can be ordered from AARP Fulfillment, 1909 K Street NW, Washington, D.C. 20049.

40

SURGICAL CORRECTION
OF JOINTS

The great majority of people with arthritis do not need surgery; for those who do, it is a last resort. However, surgery can be a welcome procedure that brings relief from pain. By the time people elect to have surgery, their condition, and their pain, has usually gone on for a very long time.

Tremendous advances have been made in joint replacement surgery, which rheumatologist Dr. Lawrence Shulman calls an "unequivocal success in removing pain and, in some patients, improving function very significantly."

If your physician suggests that you have surgery, it is always a good step to get a second opinion. Medicare covers the cost of a second opinion for elective surgery. If the second opinion disagrees with the first, Medicare also covers the cost of the third opinion. Medicare offers a second opinion hotline through which you can locate a specialist in your area. The number is (800) 638-6833; in Maryland, (800) 492-6603.

The Arthritis Foundation offers a free booklet, "Arthritis Surgery Information to Consider," which may be obtained from your local Arthritis Foundation chapter or the central office (Key 49).

Benefits of joint surgery: Among the reasons you may choose to have surgery for arthritis are these:

- relief of pain. This is the major reason people with arthritis choose surgery.
- better mobility.
- freer joint movement.

- returning use of a joint.
- cosmetic improvement to joints.

Types of joint surgery: There are a number of types of surgical procedures for arthritis. They include:

- *Arthrodesis.*Arthrodesis is the surgical fusion of joints. You may also hear this procedure referred to as "artificial ankylosis." Fusion relieves pain at the expense of loss of flexibility. The wrist, ankle, thumb, and neck are among the joints that can be fused.

- *Arthroplasty.*The technique reconstructs joints by rebuilding parts of the joint or replacing them with an artificial body part. Total hip replacement is now very successful. The ends of bones can also be resurfaced when cartilage is gone and bone is damaged.

- *Arthroscopy.*Arthroscopy is microsurgery in which the surgeon looks inside a joint with an arthroscope to perform diagnostic exploratory surgery. Debris can be removed from joints, as can bone spurs.

- *Osteotomy.*In this procedure, deformities are corrected by cutting and resetting a bone.

- *Resection.*Resection—removing part or all of a bone—may be done in the feet, the wrist, or the thumb.

- *Synovectomy.*Removal of a diseased synovial membrane, synovectomy can be performed with an arthroscope. Unfortunately, the membrane sometimes grows back.

A 1988 survey of 14,000 orthopedic surgeons found that more than one quarter of cases treated by them involve the knee. Other joints treated frequently are the spine (18 percent); the hip (16 percent); the foot (13 percent); and the hand and elbow-shoulder (12 percent each).[29]

----

[29]"Knee Treatment Tops Survey," *Arthritis Today,* July-August, 1990, p. 17.

When considering surgery: Most of the surgical procedures done on arthritic joints are safe regardless of the patient's age. A Mayo Clinic study that looked at whether surgery was risky for people in older age groups concluded that age should not be a deterrent to having surgery; in fact, the survival rate of the study's older participants was comparable to that of their peers who did not have surgery.[30]

At the same time, however, normal aging-related changes and diseases that are more common later in life, particularly heart problems, can sometimes make surgery more of a concern for older people. Here are some tips for picking a surgeon from the National Institute on Aging.[31]

- When choosing a surgeon, check to see if he or she has been certified by a board such as the American Board of Orthopaedic Surgery. Surgeons who are board certified have had a number of years of training in dealing with certain diseases and have passed the examination for their speciality. Don't hesitate to call the doctor's office and ask for this information. Your state and local medical society and the hospital where the surgeon operates should also be able to verify his or her qualifications.

- Another way of checking a surgeon's qualifications is to see if he or she is a Fellow of the American College of Surgeons. The letters F.A.C.S. after the surgeon's name indicate that he or she has passed an evaluation of surgical training and skills as well as ethical fitness.

- Choose an experienced surgeon who operates several times a week. (According to the American Academy of Orthopaedic Surgeons, the average orthopedic surgeon performs 24.5 surgical procedures a month.)

[30]"Too Old for Surgery?" *Arthritis Today,* January-February 1990.
[31]Adapted from *Age Pages,* National Institute on Aging.

- Get a second opinion. For information on when and why you should consider getting a second opinion, write to the Health Care Financing Administration for the brochure "Thinking of Having Surgery?" The address is Surgery, Dept. of Health and Home Services, Washington DC 20201.

Ask questions: Before undergoing a surgical procedure, you will be asked to sign a statement giving consent for the operation. It is important that you discuss all your concerns about your condition and the operation with your surgeon before you sign this statement. The following information might be helpful.

- What does the doctor say your problem is?
- What is the operation the doctor plans to do?
- What will happen if you don't have the operation?
- What will happen if you do have the operation?
- Are there other forms of treatment that could be tried before surgery?
- What are the risks of surgery?
- How long will the recovery period be and what is involved?
- How much will the operation cost? Will insurance cover all the costs, including special tests?
- How much experience has the surgeon had with this particular operation?
- What percent of the operations were successful?
- Who will administer the anesthesia? Is the doctor or nurse anesthetist experienced in treating older adults?
- How will the operation affect your lifestyle? Are there any activities you will not be able to do after surgery?

41

QUACK REMEDIES

Selling quack remedies for health problems such as arthritis is big business. Every year consumers spend $10 billion on bogus health products and remedies, paying good money for such fake "cures" as sitting in uranium mines and taking extracts from New Zealand green-lipped mussels or snake venom (which can result in death). Some of these products may be undergoing scientific study, but they are not considered safe and effective until sound scientific scrutiny has shown that there are no serious side effects and that they work.

Quack remedies make claims for a product or service that misrepresent what it can do. There is no scientific basis for such claims. A copper bracelet is jewelry—until it is sold as an arthritis cure. Then it is quackery.

The common image of the quack who sells bogus remedies is the "snake oil" salesman of yesteryear traveling from town to town peddling potions and elixirs. Today, quacks often dress in hospital "whites" and list meaningless impressive-looking initials after their names. They frequently target older adults. According to a study by the U.S. House of Representatives Select Committee on Aging, 60 percent of all victims of health fraud are older persons, although the elderly make up only 12 percent of the population. Arthritis sufferers are particularly susceptible to quackery because the pain and inflammation associated with the disease comes and goes, so that during periods of remission the quack can claim that the treatment is working.

Lack of regulation: The Arthritis Foundation estimates that for every dollar spent on legitimate arthritis research, $25 is spent by victims on products that claim to help the problem and do not. The sale of quack remedies is flourishing because they are not effectively regulated and any existing regulations are poorly enforced. Quacks fall through the cracks in the federal and state legal system. In addition, most medical and professional licensing boards regulate the practices of health professionals—but most quacks are not members of medical boards that can take corrective action against them. Those who have nonmedical licenses, such as a license to practice naturopathy, are usually not policed by their governing organizations. Most quacks do not have legitimate degrees or licenses of any kind, although they may try to pass themselves off with titles such as "nutritionist" or "doctor of naturopathy." These charlatans do not fall under the jurisdiction of any regulatory board, and their actions usually go unchecked until their abuses are so blatant they attract the attention of a federal agency such as the Food and Drug Administration. Then it is too late for many victims.

Examples of quack remedies: Some products and treatments sold by quacks, such as copper bracelets and sitting in uranium mines, are not dangerous. Others, such as fish oil and bee venom, are being studied; their effects are suspect but have not yet been confirmed. Still others, such as DMSO and snake venom, are known to be dangerous and can result in death.

The following are examples of quack remedies that are widely available:

- *Bee venom,* once popular in Europe, has been discredited as an arthritis "cure."
- Products advertised as *Chinese herbal medicines* have no herbs but contain drugs that may be dangerous.

136

- *Cod liver oil* contains large doses of vitamins A and D and, when taken in large amounts, can be dangerous. Oil taken by the mouth can not lubricate joints.
- *Copper bracelets* have been repeatedly condemned by the Food and Drug Administration and the Federal Trade Commission as fraudulent.
- *DMSO* (dimethyl sulfoxide) has not been shown to be effective for any form of arthritis and can be risky (Key 31).
- *Laser technology* has not been shown scientifically to be effective for arthritis.
- *Lotions and ointments* can provide some temporary comfort but cannot provide "deep, long-lasting relief," as is often advertised.
- *Snake venom* has not been shown to be effective for any form of arthritis and can cause death.
- *Special diets or diet supplements* such as "immune milk" (from cows injected with streptococcus and staphylococcus vaccines) or honey and vinegar can not "cure" arthritis. A 1989 report by the National Research Council warned against the overuse of such health-food supplements and cautioned that the following also might be harmful: fiber, lecithin, vitamins, minerals, amino acids, and protein powders.
- It is now illegal for *vibrating machines* to advertise that they prevent or cure arthritis.
- *Zinc and copper supplements* may cause serious side effects.
- Valid scientific studies have *not* been performed on *alfalfa, biofeedback, electrical devices, magnetic bracelets, magnets, New Zealand green-lipped mussel extracts, radioactive gadgets, red ant venom, seaweed, snake venom, uranium mines, vaccine therapy, and yucca.*

Any quack remedy is harmful, even if it does not have serious side effects, because precious time and money are lost while the victim could be receiving effective treatment. According to the Arthritis Foundation, to be considered legitimate, arthritis treatments must show in scientific studies that they are safe and that they accomplish at least one of the following:

- pain reduction.
- inflammation reduction.
- minimization of joint damage.
- improvement in mobility and independence.

Detecting quack remedies: The following tip-offs to health quackery and unproven remedies have been adapted from the Arthritis Foundation and the National Institute on Aging. A "cure" or remedy is probably quackery if it:

- was developed by a so-called doctor, nutritionist, or other practitioner who does not have a traditional degree. Many have imposing-looking credentials, which are not authentic, listed after their names.
- claims to work for all kinds of arthritis. No remedy could work for all 100-plus kinds of arthritis. Treatments vary for each type.
- uses case histories and testimonials from a small number of people without scientific study.
- cites only one study. A number of scientists must be able to repeat a study and get similar results for a treatment to be proven effective.
- cites a study without a control group.
- comes without directions for use.
- does not list contents.
- has no warnings about side effects.
- claims to be harmless or natural.
- is promoted by statements such as "based on a secret formula," or "cures" arthritis (there is no cure for arthritis). In addition, if it is available from only one source or is promoted exclusively through the media,

books, or mail order without having been reported in scientific journals, it is a quack remedy.

The following measures help you avoid being taken advantage of by quackery.

- Choose a health professional wisely. Ask a trusted physician, a hospital associated with a medical school, or a medical association for referrals.

- To inquire about a doctor, call the state medical board to see if complaints have been made about him or her. To inquire about a practitioner with a non-medical degree, contact the Better Business Bureau.

- Stay away from any product that uses the word "secret," "breakthrough," "natural," or "cure."

- Don't buy vitamins or minerals prescribed by a so-called professional, whether they are sold through the mail or in his or her office.

- Check out arthritis treatments with the Arthritis Foundation, the Better Business Bureau, the Federal Trade Commission, U.S. Postal Service, or the Food and Drug Administration (FDA). They all investigate health fraud and provide free material to the public about quackery.

- Stay away from products that say "FDA approved" or "endorsed by the government." Such advertising is illegal. Neither the Food and Drug Administration nor any other government agency officially approves or endorses any product.

42

ADJUSTING TO LIMITATIONS—SUPPORT GROUPS AND ARTHRITIS SELF MANAGEMENT

Self-help groups are made up of people who come together voluntarily for help in dealing with common problems and needs and who share tips and offer emotional support. Such groups have become increasingly more popular in the last couple of decades. They are generally free or ask for a small donation to cover expenses.

Arthritis self-help groups sponsored by the Arthritis Foundation are often referred to as arthritis clubs. Members get together once a month to help each other cope with chronic illness. The leaders are trained by the foundation. For example, you might attend your local group this month and pick up a tip from another member on the most effective eye drops for Sjögren's syndrome. At the same time, you might give emotional support to a friend who is facing elective surgery similar to a procedure that you recently went through. You might also get information on the newest research findings about arthritis, sign up for an exercise class, and collect a new pamphlet that interests you.

Arthritis clubs have a variety of names. In your area they might be called ACT (Arthritis—Caring Together), COPE (Communications, Openness, Problem-solving, Empathy), or the Arthritis Support Group. Arthritis Foundation chapters offer other programs important for arthritis management. Here is a list of the most popular programs:

The Arthritis Self-Help Course (ASHC): Local Arthritis Foundation chapters offer a specific six-week self-help course to help members assume responsibility for the daily care of their arthritis. The course gives people with arthritis the knowledge and skills they need to take a more active part in their arthritis care. There is a small charge, and your physician must sign a consent form for you to take the course. Among other things, the course teaches the basic aspects of arthritis and joint anatomy, principles of exercise that provide an opportunity to practice stretching and strengthening exercises, and the appropriate utilization of arthritis medications. It also encourages informed decisions about the use of special diets or nontraditional forms of treatment.

Partners in Arthritis Lay Support (PALS): This program introduces people who would like a "pal" to talk to about their arthritis to volunteers who have arthritis.

People with Arthritis Can Exercise (PACE): This program, which was discussed in Key 32, includes exercises designed specifically for people with arthritis. Two levels of the program are available—basic and advanced.

The Arthritis Aquatics Program: This program also is covered in detail in Key 32. It offers recreational exercises in a heated pool. You can actually do more in water with less pain because of the buoyancy of the water.

Systemic Lupus Erythematosus Self-Help Course: The Arthritis Foundation also offers a seven-week, 18-hour self-help class for people with lupus. The course focuses on sharing experiences with others and learning how to increase your sense of control and decrease fatigue, pain, and depression.

The Lupus Foundation: The Lupus Foundation of America also offers valuable lupus management programs through its chapters in every state and most major cities. They provide education, referral, and support services to those suffering from lupus, as well as to their families. To locate the chapter closest to you, write or call the foundation's central office (Key 49).

If your area does not have the right group for you: If your area does not offer the type of group you are interested in, you might want to start your own. Most local Arthritis Foundation chapters keep a list of people interested in starting groups.

43

ADJUSTING TO LIMITATIONS—HOME HEALTH CARE SERVICES

Health professionals providing help at home range from nurses to occupational therapists. Their services are invaluable if limitations strike or after surgery.

Physicians initiate the homecare/homemaker services, authorize a coordinated plan of treatment, and periodically review the delivery and effectiveness of the services.

Nurses—registered nurses and licensed practical nurses—provide direct skilled nursing services, supervise other caregivers, coordinate patient care with the physician, and train family and friends so they can maintain the program when professional services are needed.

Homemaker/home health aides provide personal care such as assistance in bathing, grooming, dressing, cooking, and cleaning under the supervision of a professional.

Physical and occupational therapists play an invaluable role in home health care for arthritis patients. They may see their patients not in their homes, but at a clinic or hospital where special equipment is available. But their magic often enables the arthritis sufferer to be more independent at home and have a higher quality of life.

Physical therapists help people whose strength, ability to move, sensation, or range of motion is impaired. They may use exercise, heat, cold, water therapy or other treatments to control pain, strengthen muscles, and improve coordination.

143

Occupational therapists assist patients with handicaps to function more independently. They may also provide exercise programs; heat, cold, and whirlpool treatments to relieve pain; and hand splints and adaptive equipment to improve function and independence.

Occupational and physical therapy: Both physical and occupational therapists can help correct problems with posture, movements, and resting or sleeping. They can suggest alternative ways of doing things and provide exercises for pain.

What the physical therapist does. Physical therapists are licensed by the state and have a knowledge of anatomy and physiology. The therapist will confer with your doctor about your diagnosis and then, based on tests for problems and functioning, he or she will choose what exercise and treatment will work best. You may be able to do some exercises alone; others may require help. The therapist will also recommend any assistive devices or appliances you may need.

It is advisable that family members be present when you are working with a physical therapist so they can learn how to help you when the therapist is not present.

What the occupational therapist does. The occupational therapist will talk to your physical therapist and doctor and, after evaluating you, work with you to help increase mobility. If necessary, the therapist will also teach you how to do necessary daily activities such as getting in and out of your clothes and how to cut down on pain and protect joints. Many therapists have available models of adapted rooms such as bathrooms and kitchens, and they can teach you how to modify your own home to maintain your independence. The occupational therapist can see how accessible your living environment is, looking at everything from your ability to get up and down the stairs to reaching the cabinets in the kitchen. In most cases, occupational therapists will be able to offer suggestions to improve your functioning in your home.

Ask questions: Asking a nurse or physical therapist for advice can often prevent serious problems, even though the questions may seem silly at the time. For example, one problem that older persons with back pain often develop is "locking," or flexion contractures, in which the knees cannot be bent. Ironically, the contractures develop from using an instinctive and effective technique to relieve pain—sleeping or resting with a pillow under the knees. A nurse or other trained professional can help you avoid this kind of problem with some quick, simple tips on how to adjust the pillows properly or when not to use them.

Finding resources: There are a number of ways to locate home health care services. Your doctor or friends may be able to tell you about agencies with which they have had good experiences. (This is important because bad agencies do exist, and a personal recommendation can avoid problems.) The information and referral worker at your local office on aging is also usually a good resource for any age-related services. You will find the offices listed in the blue pages of your phone book; they go by different names in different areas so locating them may take some creativity on your part.

You also might contact the National Association of Private Geriatric Care Managers, 1315 Talbott Towers, Dayton OH 45042 (513) 222-2621 or Aging Network Services, Topaz House, Suite 907, 4400 East-West Highway, Bethesda MD 20814 (301) 657-4329. Both provide lists of their members.

44

ADJUSTING TO LIMITATIONS—USING ASSISTIVE DEVICES

Wrestling with everyday activities can be difficult when your joints are stiff and sore. Luckily, however, more and more ingenious devices are coming on the market that provide independence and mobility to even the most disabled. Just some examples are "arthwriters" that can make writing easier and more legible, "portable catapult seats" to push you up and out of your chair, and "skin-sensitive switches" that turn appliances on and off when you lightly touch a switch with your fingers. These devices represent the vanguard of a movement in innovative design which, in the not too distant future, will allow robots to prepare and serve our meals, clean our houses, and run our baths.

Many aids are available from medical supply stores, drug stores, and hardware stores and through catalogues. In addition, occupational therapists are ideal sources of information on where to locate assistive devices and how to use them. Some aids can be made at home or involve the clever use of objects designed for other purposes; for example, foam hair curlers make great grip extenders for everything from hairbrushes to spatulas, and dowels or wooden curtain rods with hooks on the end make terrific door and drawer openers.

It is a good idea to go through your living space, with an occupational therapist if possible, and examine every storage, work, sitting, and sleeping space to see how it could be more efficient. Are your kitchen utensils in drawers that are hard to open? Put them on a low shelf where they are easy to reach. Do you have trouble going up and down stairs? You may want to consider a stair lift. Is it difficult to carry items from room to room? Try a cart to wheel groceries from cabinet to cabinet and to move your evening snack from the kitchen to the TV room. Figure 44-1 shows some of the things that you can do in your home to improve efficiency and save on joints.

Some assistive devices are covered in part by Medicare and other insurance, provided your doctor prescribes them. Check with your insurance carrier first to make sure that the device you are purchasing is reimbursable under its guidelines.

Here is a selected list of items that you can purchase in stores or order through specialty catalogues. The list is by no means exhaustive; new products are coming on the market all the time. You may want to get on the mailing list of some of the best catalogues for information on new items. (A short list of catalogues appears at the end of this Key). In addition, an organization called Abledata maintains an exhaustive database on assistive devices. Information on how to reach them is provided in Key 49.

General aids:
Arthwriters allow you to write with arm movement rather than finger movement.
Assisto-seats push you up and out of your chair.
Carts on wheels
Clip-it-cutters are useful for cutting items from a newspaper or magazine with one hand.
Cordless telephones
Doorknob extension handles
Door operators allow easy opening of any type of door and come in a variety of designs.
Dowels with hooks at the end are for opening doors.

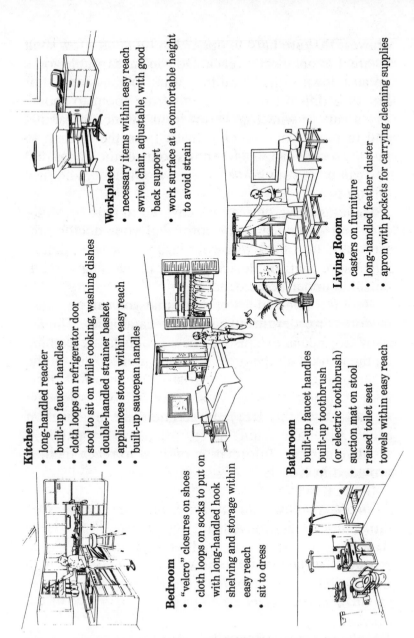

Workplace
- necessary items within easy reach
- swivel chair, adjustable, with good back support
- work surface at a comfortable height to avoid strain

Kitchen
- long-handled reacher
- built-up faucet handles
- cloth loops on refrigerator door
- stool to sit on while cooking, washing dishes
- double-handled strainer basket
- appliances stored within easy reach
- built-up saucepan handles

Living Room
- casters on furniture
- long-handled feather duster
- apron with pockets for carrying cleaning supplies

Bedroom
- "velcro" closures on shoes
- cloth loops on socks to put on with long-handled hook
- shelving and storage within easy reach
- sit to dress

Bathroom
- built-up faucet handles
- built-up toothbrush (or electric toothbrush)
- suction mat on stool
- raised toilet seat
- towels within easy reach

Figure 44–1: Illustration courtesy of The Arthritis Foundation, *Taking Care, Protecting Your Joints and Saving Energy.*

Dycem™ grippers are nonslip pads for everything from keeping telephones to dishes in place.

Electric scissors

Electric staplers

Foam hair curlers improve gripping when put on the end of utensils.

Giant pushbutton telephone adapters are large buttons that clamp over regular-size telephone buttons.

Gripper tape is excellent for cushioning handles.

Handclasps with a dowel attached are helpful for activities like typing and using a pushbutton telephone.

Head sets for telephones

Key extenders

Lamp switch extension levers simplify turning a lamp on and off.

Light switch extenders make turning lights on and off easier.

Long-handled tongs are good for reaching faraway objects.

Pillbox alarms are good for keeping track of your medication times (some models play music).

Phone holders attach to any surface and hold the phone at any angle. Use with a "fone flipper," which controls phone connections with a lever so there is no need to pick up a receiver.

Portable catapult seats push you up and out of your chair; models come in varying weights and with carrying handles.

Reachers will grab items more than an arm's length away.

Remote control extension cords are for any type of appliance.

Shoulder attachments for telephones

Skin-sensitive appliance switches enable you to turn appliances on and off by lightly touching a central switch with your fingers.

Speaker phones
Splints that hold writing utensils
Telephones with automatic dialers
Telephones with large buttons
Voice-activated light switches

Dressing aids:

Button extenders

Button hooks

Dressing sticks and hooks are great for pulling on clothes and pulling zippers up or down.

Elastic shoelaces stay tied once they are in place, and there is no need to retie them.

Front-closing bras

Lacelocks eliminate the need to tie shoelaces.

Long-handled shoehorns

Shoe removers are plastic platforms that help you take shoes off without bending over.

Stocking and sock helpers help pull up and take off stockings and socks.

Velcro™ can be artfully hidden behind buttons to make dressing easier; many catalogues offer clothing with Velcro™ closures.

Wheelchair skirts

Zipper laces make fastening shoes easier.

Zipper loops and pulls help with small zipper tabs that are difficult to grasp.

Grooming aids:

Combs and brushes with jointed handle extensions minimize arm movements: many other adapted types of handles are also available.

Cuff-handled extensions eliminate the need to grasp items.

Hairbrushes with Velcro™ handles fit easily in your hand.

Suction boards with nail clippers and files attached allow you to move your nail against the file instead of having to grasp the file with the other hand; simplify movement for clipping nails.

Velcro™ hair rollers eliminate the need for pins or clips.

Wall-mounted hair driers eliminate the need to hold the drier in your hands.

Bathing aids:

Bathtub inserts include seats.

Footbaths for cleaning and hydrotherapy can also be used for pain relief of hands and arms.

Grab bars should be in every bathroom, regardless of the occupants' age, to provide safety when getting in and out of the bathtub or shower. They can be installed on the wall or attached to the side of the bathtub.

Gooseneck mounted mirrors eliminate the need to hold the mirror to see difficult angles, such as the back of the head.

Long-handled combs, brushes, and sponges help to reach high and low when range of movement is limited; back brushes come in styles that curve around the back.

Long-handled sponges

Shower hoses are useful for rinsing off when sitting in the tub.

Shower mitts with a pocket to hold soap

Soap-on-a-rope keeps the soap from falling out of reach.

Suction-mounted nail brushes allow you to move your nails against the brush instead of having to grasp it with the other hand.

Transfer benches are useful for getting in and out of the tub.

Tub and shower benches allow you to sit while bathing.

Toileting aids:

Bidets or bidet attachments for toilets are for cleaning with a stream of water; some come with a burst of warm air for drying.

Hygiene aids for use after eliminating provide help for those with limited arm movement.

Multipurpose commode chairs with wheels can be moved anywhere and will fit over a toilet.

Raised toilet seats may be placed over the toilet.

Toilet paper tongs

Toilet safety frames provide safety when sitting down and getting up from the toilet.

Dental hygiene aids:

Dental floss holders

Electric toothbrushes

Suction-mounted denture brushes

Toothbrushes and razors with jointed handle extensions

Toothpaste in pumps

Water-Piks™ make deep cleaning easier.

Food preparation aids:

Angled coffee pots and tea pots permit pouring without lifting the pot.

Carton grips

Curved utensils (including a curved knife) are particularly useful. Use your thumb on top of the handle so cutting pressure comes from the upper part of the arm.

Cutting boards with nails for holding food are easy to make or can be purchased.

Dycem™ pads hold almost anything in place.

Electric knives

Folding pan holders secure a pan in place on top of the stove.

Food processors allow easier stirring, cutting, and mixing.

Food scissors are often easier to use than a knife.

Knob extension turners permit easier turning of stove knobs.

Lightweight pots and pans: when joints are painful and stiff, occupational therapists recommend that you trade in your heavy cookware for those that are easier to hold.

Hoop aprons eliminate tying apron strings.

Jar openers allow you to grip the lid with both hands.

Oven shovels are for putting things in the oven and taking them out without straining. They are also great for tucking sheets under a mattress.

Slitting devices are for opening bags.

Steamer baskets that fit inside pots make easier draining possible.

Sponges on handles are good for getting to far-away places.

Suction cups stabilize bowls, pots, and pans.

Suction vegetable brushes let you move the vegetable against the brush instead of having to grasp it with the other hand.

Two-handled pots and pans permit easier grasping.

Vegetable and fruit holders are for one-handed slicing.

Wheel knives allow easier cutting.

Zyliss jar openers make opening tubes and jars easier.

Eating and drinking aides:

Bent glass straws

Boards with spikes for holding food

Cuff-mounted utensils, often called universal cuffs, are for holding utensils.

Rimmed dishes keep food from spilling and provide leverage for eating utensils.

Double-handled cups are easier to hold.

Dycem™ is nonslide material for putting under plates, bowls, etc.

Clip-on straw holders

Electric knives

Food guards keep food from spilling and provide leverage for eating utensils. They are removable for cleaning.

Glass holders come in tilting holders that allow you to drink without leaning over.

Invalid cups can be used from a reclining position.

Rocker knives permit one-handed cutting.

Rubber suction cups steady dishes.

Sandwich holders make easier grasping possible.

Swivel utensils are more manageable because the swivel motion keeps the utensils level.

Two-handled mugs permit easier holding.

Utensils with extension handles

Weighted cups and eating utensils add stability.

Housekeeping aids:

Electric brooms

Electric pot scrubbers

Foot mops allow you to mop while you walk.

Long-handled dustpans

Self-wringing mops

Sponge mops with automatic wringers

Suction-mounted brushes remain stationary while you move the object against it. They are available in various shapes and sizes.

Zippered mesh bags and long tongs aid the removal of small items from the washing machine.

Hobbies, recreation, and leisure time aids:

Attachable embroidery frames can be attached to tables or chairs.

Automatic threading machines

Book holders come in overhead models.

Book turners can be attached to a cuff.

Fishing rod holders permit one-handed fishing.

Garden knee pads fasten to the legs with leather straps.

Gardening "scoots" are tractor-style seats on wheels that can roll over grass and soil.

Knitting needle holders permit one-handed knitting.

Long-reach fruit and flower pickers

Jumbo game sets allow easier handling for a full range of games from dice to backgammon.

No-hold magnifiers hang from your neck and brace against your chest.

Playing-card holders enable you to see all of the hand that is dealt to you.

Playing-card shufflers.

Special bowling balls have a release handle that helps propel the ball. Bowling ball ramps are also available for people in wheelchairs.

Special pool cues are available for people with only one functional hand.

Universal support arm attachments are for mounting such things as binoculars and hobby equipment to chairs.

Aids for the bed:

Bed wedges, backrests, nonslip cushions

Blanket supports keep sheets away from the body.

Book holders

Fabrian™ Reading/Writing Aids make it possible to read and write without using hands.

Nova™ patient transfer systems will be available soon and will transfer you from your bed to a wheelchair.

Overhead book holders

Prism glasses allow reading and watching TV with the head flat.

Talking books are books on audiotape.

Tilting tray tables aid writing.

Trapeze bars let you pull yourself up in bed.

Aids to getting around:

Adaptive devices for cars can be installed by companies located in most major cities. Examples include special brake and gas pedals and hydraulic lifts.

Canes include four-footed models for stability.

Car cushions to support the lower back include Sacro Ease™ seats and the Bottoms Up Posture Seat™.

Car door openers

Elevators can be installed in closet space.

Glideabouts are seats on rollers that glide over floors and through doorways and halls.

Modified cars and vans are available for mobile persons with disabilities and people in wheelchairs.

Ramps are available in portable models.

Stair lifts are mechanical chairs that take you up and down stairs. They are available in indoor and outdoor models.

Swivel cushions are good for getting in and out of a car.

Tools for unlocking car doors

Three-wheeled motorized scooters usually fit through doorways.

Reacher canes give support when walking and also pick up objects.

Walkers are available in standard, folding, seated, and three-wheeled models.

Catalogs:

Access to Recreation, 2509 East Thousand Oaks Blvd., Thousand Oaks CA 91362.

Comfortably Yours, 2515 East 43rd Street, Chattanooga TN 37422 (201) 368-0400.

Enrichments, P.O. Box 579, Hinsdale IL 60521 (800) 343-9742, in Illinois, Alaska, and Hawaii call (312) 325-1625.

Fashion Able, Box S, Rocky Hill NJ 08553 (609) 989-9700.

Sears Home Health Care Catalog, from your closest Sears store.

45

PAYING FOR HEALTH CARE

After age 65 your primary source of health insurance for arthritis-related medical expenses is likely to be Medicare. Ninety-seven percent of all 65-plus Americans are enrolled in the program. However, because Medicare covers less than half of the total costs of health care for older adults, other cost-saving options are also important. They include purchasing supplemental health insurance, joining a Medicare HMO, applying for Medicaid, using veterans' benefits, and taking advantage of tax deductions. This Key provides basic information about these options, as well as what options are available if you have not yet reached the age of eligibility for Medicare.

Medicare: Medicare is a two-part system that provides health insurance to qualified individuals over age 65. Medicare Part A helps pay for hospital room and board costs, skilled nursing facilities, home health care, and hospice care. Part B helps to pay physicians and other medical service providers, whether in or out of the hospital. It also covers part of the costs of the wide range of medical services people use when they are not patients in hospitals, including outpatient visits, physical therapy, laboratory tests, medical equipment (such as wheelchairs or oxygen), and home health visits. Neither Part A nor B cover the cost of long-term care in a nursing home or at home.

Eligibility for Medicare: If you are a Social Security or Railroad Retirement beneficiary, you will receive a Medicare card in the mail three months before your

65th birthday. There is no charge for Part A, but you will have to pay a premium for Part B benefits. If you decide to delay enrollment in Part B you can sign up at a later date, but you will have to pay a substantial penalty that increases with time.

Anyone not eligible for Medicare through Social Security or Railroad Retirement can pay a monthly premium and receive benefits. For an application, contact your closest Social Security office.

Financial assistance for low-income Medicare beneficiaries. If your income falls below the national poverty level, your state is required by federal law to provide you with some assistance in paying for Medicare's premiums, deductibles, and co-insurance. To be eligible, you must not be eligible for Medicaid. For information about the program, contact your state or local social service office and ask about the "Medicaid buy-in."

Health Maintenance Organizations (HMOs): Medicare HMOs provide all services that Medicare recipients are entitled to, as well as some additional services. For example, many HMOs cover the full costs of impatient hospitalization, including the deductible. Other services may include immunizations, prescription drugs at reduced cost, and routine eye care. The costs and benefits of HMOs vary from plan to plan, so it is important to do comparison shopping with the plans in your area.

The Medicare HMOs in your area may charge a monthly fee. However, this is generally less than the co-insurance and deductible amounts that you would pay if you were not a member of an HMO. In addition, Medicare HMOs have lock-in features, meaning that neither Medicare nor the HMO will pay for medical care anywhere but in the HMO. Exceptions are made in emergencies or when an HMO makes a referral because it does not provide a specific service.

To be eligible for a Medicare HMO you must be

enrolled in Medicare's Part B, which means you will continue to pay the premium. Also, you must either have Medicare Part A or pay a higher charge to the HMO. You must also live in the HMO's geographical area for at least nine months of the year.

Medicare recipients cannot be denied enrollment in an HMO because of advanced age or any "pre-existing medical condition," no matter how severe, with the exception of persons with end-stage kidney failure. In addition, all Medicare HMOs are required to have at least one 30-day open enrollment period every year during which individuals may join.

Supplemental health insurance: The purpose of Medicare supplemental policies, or medigap policies, as they are commonly called, is to fill in the gaps that Medicare does not cover. Policies that are called Medicare supplements cover services only after Medicare pays first. This is an important point for Medicare beneficiaries with arthritis, many of whom have heavy medical expenses for services that Medicare does not cover, such as prescription drugs. Most medigap plans do cover co-payments and deductibles. Some policies add additional benefits, but they also have substantially higher premiums.

A note of caution when shopping for Medicare supplements—the best policies are not necessarily those offered by organizations for older adults such as the American Association of Retired Persons. In fact, *Consumer Reports* rated AARP's best policy fifth in the nation; four other widely available policies provided more coverage for a lower cost.

Medicaid benefits: If you cannot afford supplemental insurance or are not eligible for Medicare, you should investigate the possibility of receiving help from Medicaid. Medicaid is a government-financed assistance program that pays for medical care for people who have limited income and cannot afford insurance. In many states, if you receive Supplemental Security Income you automatically qualify for Medicaid. If you are eligible for both Medicare and Medicaid, Medicaid will probably pay for your Medicare premiums, deductibles, and co-insurance amounts. If you have Medicaid, you do not need supplemental health insurance.

To be eligible for Medicaid you must meet certain income and asset tests. You must also be a resident of the state in which you are applying. To apply, contact your state department of social services.

Veterans benefits: If you are eligible for veterans' benefits, you may receive more comprehensive coverage than you would under Medicare. For example, you may qualify for treatment in a nursing home, which Medicare does not cover. However, veterans with service-related disabilities always receive priority for services ahead of other veterans with medical needs, so depending on your medical history, your name could be at the bottom of the list for benefits. Local Departments of Veterans Affairs and organizations such as the Veterans of Foreign Wars and the American Legion handle applications for veterans' benefits.

Insurance options prior to becoming a Medicare recipient: If you are between retirement and age 65 and you have the option of continuing group insurance through your present or former employer, this is generally the best alternative until you become eligible for Medicare. Purchasing individual insurance is usually an expensive last resort. However, if this is your only option, take it. It is dangerous to go without any kind of health insurance at all, so it is better to swallow the costs than to go uninsured.

Disability benefits: If you are under age 65, are unable to work because of a disability, and have enough "work credit" under Social Security, you may be eligible for Social Security's disability program. Once you receive such benefits for 24 months you will automatically receive Medicare Part A. To receive Medicare Part B, you must enroll and pay a monthly premium.

If you are not eligible for Social Security's disability benefits and you are not able to work, you may qualify for Supplemental Security Income (SSI). SSI recipients receive Medicaid. For information on both programs, ask your local Social Security office for a copy of a pamphlet called "Filing for Social Security or Supplemental Security Income Disability Benefits."

Medical expense deductions for federal taxes: All medical expenses that exceed 7.5 percent of your gross income may be deducted from your income taxes. You can deduct only that portion of your expenses for which you alone are responsible. In other words, you cannot deduct expenses that were reimbursed by Medicare or supplemental insurance. The following expenses are deductible:

- prescription drugs and insulin (not over-the-counter drugs or vitamins).
- doctor's fees.
- hospital expenses (but not personal expenses).
- Transportation to and from the doctor's or dentist's office or other place of treatment.
- medical insurance premiums.
- medical supplies and equipment.
- certain lodging and meals away from home in connection with medical care.
- therapy and treatment of specific medical problems.
- care in a nursing home as long as medical care is one of the reasons for the stay. When residence in a nursing home is to provide assistance for a chronic problem, only the medical care portion of the stay is deductible. Room and board are *not* deductible.
- drug abuse and alcoholism clinics.

- home nursing care when connected with a physical disability or neurological disorder.

Deductions may also be taken for a range of expenses such as false teeth, hearing aids, artificial limbs, braille typewriters, and special telephones and equipment for the deaf.

Dependent care tax credits: Twenty-nine states now have some form of dependent care tax credit. In addition, a small federal tax credit is available for working individuals who provide care for dependents such as elderly parents. Individuals must meet all of the following requirements:

- Husband and wife must be working or looking for work.
- The individual or couple filing the claim must be paying one-half of the household expenses.
- The expenses must be incurred to enable the person(s) filing the claim to work.

In addition, the older dependent person must be:

- a mentally or physically incapacitated person who is claimed as a dependent.
- a spouse who is physically or mentally handicapped and unable to care for himself or herself.

The following caps apply to the credit:

- No more than $2,400 may be counted for one dependent and $4,800 for two or more dependents.
- The deduction is limited to the lower amount of income earned by either spouse. (Disabled spouses are treated as if they earned $200 per month.)
- The deduction is limited to a percentage of income ranging from 20 to 30 percent.

46

NEW HORIZONS IN RESEARCH AND TREATMENT

What does the future look like for arthritis sufferers? Will we ever be able to predict who will get arthritis and why? Will we be able to treat inflammation? To control the immune system? To regenerate and repair cartilage?

The answers to all of these questions is yes. Arthritis-related research has produced spectacular advances in the last decade, and many more advances are on the horizon.

That's the good news. The down side is that most of these advances are a couple of decades away. Arthritis is very difficult to research, and progress comes at a snail's pace. According to Dr. Arthur Grayzel of the Arthritis Foundation, "Arthritis is a difficult subject to study because you don't have much access to the tissue. You can study skin and other systems with age much more easily than you can study cartilage." In addition, research takes a long time because arthritic conditions progress very slowly.

The following synopsis of the most recent research findings and their implications for the future is based in part on interviews with Dr. Grayzel and with Dr. Lawrence E. Shulman, director of the National Institute of Arthritis and Musculoskeletal and Skin Diseases.

Agents to retard bone loss: A number of new findings have advanced research in this area. First, new agents that retard bone loss are being discovered. Prime among these are the hormones estrogen and progesterone. In addition, the drug etridonate, which is currently used to treat Paget's disease, has been found to be very effective.

Third, science has been able to establish the importance of calcium and vitamin D in preventing bone loss. One study shows that women who take less than the daily recommended amount of calcium have much less bone mass than women who take the recommended daily dosage. Fourth, calcitonin has been also found to retard bone loss. (However, for practical use, it is very expensive.)

What is ahead in research in this area? Scientists are working on locating an effective agent that can "turn on" bone that has been lost.

The immune system and inflammation: According to Dr. Grayzel, in the next century naturally occurring substances will be used to control the immune system and inflammation. Grayzel says: "These agents are the hope of the next decade or two."

About a dozen substances are being studied presently, including interferon. Most are being studied for cancer and the effects of acute infection but may have other applications.

Dr. Grayzel points out that it does not look like any one of these natural substances alone will do the trick, because the body uses them in combination. A major research priority is to learn what combinations are effective against arthritis.

Cartilage: One hope for treating osteoarthritis is that research will discover a way of triggering cartilage regeneration and repair. Until recently it was assumed that this was next to impossible and that, once cartilage was damaged, it could not repair itself. Now scientists are starting to isolate growth substances for cartilage, as well as those that inhibit cartilage regeneration.

Surgery: Extraordinary advances in surgery have taken place recently, particularly for the knee and the hip. Investigators are now trying to improve the materials used in artificial joints and are making refinements in how they are glued in place. What is ahead? Scientists are working on effective finger and ankle joint replacements.

Infectious agents: One course of investigation for finding the cause of some types of arthritis involves the search for infectious agents that may act as triggers. Researchers have studied a bacterium that is associated with a type of arthritis called sterile inflammatory polyarthropathy. This type of arthritis affects people with a particular genetic type called HLA-B27; the researchers found that part of the genetic material in the bacterium is identical to the HLA-B27 genetic material. The identical genetic structure may play a key role in certain types of arthritis.[32]

A molecular marker for osteoarthritis: Researchers have recently discovered a genetic marker for osteoarthritis that could lead to improved diagnosis and treatment. The marker is a defect in type 2 collagen, which is a large molecule that is important in giving cartilage its strength and stability. The defect results in cartilage that is weak and that breaks down early in life.

The marker was originally found in three generations of one family and subsequently has been found in other families. Further study is taking place in this area. According to Dr. Grayzel, this finding has changed the way that scientists think about osteoarthritis. Research is beginning on searching for defects in other molecules that contribute to the condition.

A molecular marker for lupus and rheumatoid arthritis: Using mice with autoimmune diseases,

[32] *Arthritis Today,* "Scientific Frontier," p. 8, January-February 1990.

165

researchers at the University of California at Irvine have found a defect in immune cells called "double-negative" T cells. If they find a comparable defect in humans, it may be possible to develop a drug to control the range of autoimmune diseases, including lupus and rheumatoid arthritis.

New medications: A big advance in pharmaceutical help for rheumatoid arthritis is the effectiveness of low doses of the drug methotrexate (see Key 28). In addition, in the future, a brand-new class of medications may prove helpful against the inflammation of arthritis. The drugs, 5-lipoxygenase inhibitors, work by inhibiting leukotrienes, which cause inflammation and are involved in the breaking down of collagen. A new drug in this class is now being tested on humans. In addition, two other types of medication have shown promise. First, a new genetically engineered treatment called interleukin-2 fusion toxin has produced dramatic improvement for rheumatoid arthritis in early stages. Second, two drugs known as butoxamine and ICI 118, which work by blocking part of the nervous system, have prevented arthritis in animals.

A new test for Lyme disease: Current tests for Lyme disease are not always accurate, leading people to think that they do not have the disease when they do. A new test is presently being developed at the University of California at Davis that would identify a specific protein that causes symptoms. Once the test is developed, it may also lead to a vaccine against the disease.

Fish oils: According to a report in *Geriatrics* magazine, several research centers have studied the effects of supplementing regular medication and diet with fish oils.[33] Fish oils are omega-3 fatty acids, which are poly-

---

[33] Joel Kremer, "Severe rheumatoid arthritis: Current options in drug therapy," *Geriatrics,* December 1990, p. 47.

166

unsaturated fatty acids derived from certain species of fish. They appear to affect certain imflammatory and immune biological systems. In addition, fish oils appear to be nontoxic. However, further studies are needed before we start supplementing diets with fish oil.

Research benefiting women: Dr. Grayzel emphasizes that arthritis affects a disproportionate number of women and that scientific advances in this area would have tremendous benefit for them. It is interesting to note that the National Institute of Arthritis and Musculoskeletal and Skin Diseases (NIAMS), part of the National Institutes of Health (NIH), is the one institute that actually uses more women than men in its studies. In most studies in other institutes, women make up less than 50 percent of subjects. In NIAMS studies, women constitute 60 to 70 percent of subjects.

The research budget: According to Don L. Riggin, president and CEO of the Arthritis Foundation, one of the foundation's major goals is to increase funding for research for arthritis, both from foundations and from the federal government. The Arthritis Foundation currently helps to support 180 research centers. Unhappily, the budget for the government's NIAMS is very tight in comparison with other government-sponsored institutes. NIAMS can fund only one in six approved grant applications, while the rate for all of NIH is one in four. In order to help increase research on arthritis, the Arthritis Foundation has begun a legislative campaign called "Arthritis Research for a New Age." To find out how you can participate, call your local chapter and request the brochure *Effective Volunteer Lobbying,* or write the national office of the Arthritis Foundation, listed in Key 49.

GLOSSARY

Angiogram a test in which dye is injected into an artery and an X-ray is taken.

Ankylosing Spondylitis a form of arthritis that attacks the spine.

Antibody a substance produced in the blood that is capable of producing a specific immunity to a germ or virus. Rheumatoid factor is an antibody.

Antinuclear antibody (or ANA) an antibody found in the blood of most lupus victims.

Arteries large blood vessels.

Arthalgia joint pain alone without the redness and swelling of arthritis.

Arthritis inflammation of the joint. However, some conditions that do not involve joint inflammation are often covered under the term arthritis.

Arthrodesis the surgical fusion of joints. Pain is relieved, but at the expense of loss of flexibility. This is also referred to as artificial ankylosis.

Arthroplasty the reconstruction of joints by rebuilding or replacement with an artificial body part.

Arthroscope a lighted, hollow instrument that can be used to perform exploratory or other surgery such as a synovectomy.

Arthroscopy a surgical procedure in which a surgeon looks inside a joint with an instrument called an arthroscope.

Articular the juncture of two bones (a joint).

Autoimmune diseases diseases that occur when the immune system attacks healthy parts of the body.

Bacterium germ. Some theories suggest that rheumatoid arthritis is triggered by a bacterium in those people with a susceptibility to it.

Biopsy the removal of a small piece of tissue for diagnosis.

Bouchard's nodes bony outgrowths at specific joints called the proximal interphalangeals (PIPs).

Bursae soft, fluid-filled sacs that separate the muscles that cross bones or other muscles.

Bursitis inflammation of the bursae.

Calcium pyrophosphate deposition disease (see pseudogout).

Cartilage a tough elastic tissue that absorbs shocks and cushions bone ends, enabling them to slide smoothly against each other.

Chronic lasting for a lifetime.

Flares periods when arthritis symptoms worsen.

Flexion contractures the inability to move a joint.

Granulomas inflammatory nodules within tissue.

Hallux valgus a minor foot disorder in which the big toe overlaps one or more other toes.

Heberdon's nodes bony outgrowths at specific joints called the distal interphalangeals (DIPs).

Hyperuricemia an excess of uric acid, a waste product, in the blood.

Infectious arthritis joint inflammation that has been caused by bacteria, viruses, or infections.

Joint aspiration the process of removing fluid and crystals from joints.

Joints the mechanisms that provide relatively friction-free motion between bones.

Inflammation a reaction by tissue to injury, evidenced by pain, swelling, heat, and redness.

Ligaments fibrous structures that attach bones.

Localized limited in effect, as opposed to a condition that affects the whole body.

Muscles elastic tissues that expand and contract to enable the body to move. They are attached to the bones with tendons.

Osteomalacia the softening of bone.

Osteoporosis an age-related condition in which bone mass decreases, causing bones to fracture easily.

Osteotomy the cutting and resetting of a bone.

Pannus a mass that forms in the joint from inflammation of the synovial membrane.

Photosensitivity extreme sensitivity to the sun, common in lupus.

Pleurisy pain on breathing.

Prostaglandins fatty acids that affect many body activities, including the excretion of stomach acid.

Pseudogout a build up of calcium pyrophosphate in the joints.

Purines waste products in food that form uric acid when the body breaks them down. Excess uric acid, in turn, leads to gout.

Raynaud's phenomenon a condition in which the feet and hands turn blue on exposure to cold.

Resection the removal of part or all of a bone.

Rheumatic disorders disorders involving tendons, muscles, and other tissues around the joints.

Rheumatoid factor a gamma globulin or antibody found in the blood and joint fluid of about 80 percent of adults with rheumatoid arthritis.

Scleroderma a chronic disease in which most victims have problems with their skin. The disease can also affect joints, blood vessels, muscles, bones, and internal organs.

Sedimentation rate ("sed rate") a laboratory test that measures how fast red blood cells sink to the bottom of a special tube.

Synovectomy the removal of a diseased synovial membrane.

Synovial fluid a liquid that moistens and nourishes the surfaces of cartilage.

Synovial membrane the thin inner lining of the capsule surrounding joints. The membrane releases synovial fluid into the space between the bones. In rheumatoid arthritis the lining becomes thickened and releases excess fluid.

Systemic a condition that affects the whole body, as opposed to a localized condition which is limited in effect.

Tendonitis inflammation of the tendons.

Tendons bands of fibrous tissue that connect muscles to bones.

Tinnitus a ringing in the ears, a common side effect of taking aspirin.

Tophi deposits of uric acid that build up in the joints and surrounding tissues.

Uricosuric drugs drugs that lower the uric acid level in the blood by increasing the amount passed in urine.

Virus organism capable of causing an infectious or contagious disease. Research suggests that rheumatoid arthritis may be triggered by a virus in those people with a susceptibility to it.

RESOURCES

Agencies and organizations: If you have arthritis, you will find a valuable resource in the Arthritis Foundation chapter closest to you (see below). Foundation chapters provide an array of valuable services such as exercise programs and self-management courses. They also supply more than 180 informative booklets and brochures free of charge. You can get a list of publications from your local chapter or from the foundation's national office.

The foundation's two goals (since 1948) are (1) to support research to find the cures for and the preventions of arthritis diseases and (2) to improve the quality of life for those affected by arthritis. The staff of the foundation works to get across the message that arthritis is a serious set of conditions, not just aches and pains—and that the Arthritis Foundation is where sufferers can find help.

The Arthritis Foundation has 600,000 members, 71 chapters, and 150 delivery points. Current dues are $20 a year, 75 cents of which goes back into programs and services. Membership includes access to services, a subscription to *Arthritis Today,* and a pharmacy discount. In addition, the foundation supports 180 research centers.

The address for inquiries to the foundation is:
PO Box 19000
Atlanta, GA 30326
The address and phone number for the national office of the foundation is:
Arthritis Foundation
1314 Spring Street NW
Atlanta, GA 30309
(404) 872-7100

(For information on how to contact Arthritis Foundation chapters, see below.)

Another important resource for information is the National Institute of Arthritis and Musculoskeletal and Skin Diseases, which is part of the National Institutes of Health. The institute is the focal point for government research on arthritis and also provides valuable information packets to the public about the numerous forms of the condition.

The address and phone number for the institute is:
National Institute of Arthritis and Musculoskeletal and Skin Diseases
Building 31, Room 4CO5
Bethesda MD 20892
(301) 496-8188

The following organizations also provide valuable information and services:
• For people with lupus:
The American Lupus Society
3914 Del Amo Blvd.
Suite 922
Torrance CA 90503
(213) 542-8891,
(800) 331-1802
The society has chapters in all states and most large cities.
• For people with Sjögren's and other moisture problems:
Moisture Seekers
29 Gateway Drive
Great Neck NY 11021
(516) 767-2866
• For people with scleroderma:
The United Scleroderma Foundation
P.O. Box 350
Watsonville CA 95077
(408) 728-2202
• To locate orthopedic surgeons:
American Academy of Orthopaedic Surgeons
222 S. Prospect Avenue
Park Ridge IL 60068
• For a database of assistive devices:
Abledata National Rehabilitation Information Center
Catholic University of America
4407 8th Street NE
Washington, DC 20017-2299

ARTHRITIS FOUNDATION CHAPTERS

Alabama Chapter
200 Vestavia Pky, #3050
Birmingham, AL 35216
(205) 979-5700

South Alabama Chapter
1720 Springhill Avenue
Mobile, AL 36604
(205) 432-7171

Alaska Unit
c/o Western Area Office
1314 Spring St., NW
Atlanta, GA 30309
(404) 872-7100

Central Arizona Chapter
711 E Missouri Ave., #116
Phoenix, AZ 85014
(602) 264-7679

Southern Arizona Chapter
6464 East Grant Road
Tucson, AZ 85715
(602) 290-9090

Arkansas Chapter
6213 Lee Avenue
Little Rock, AR 72205
(501) 664-7242

Northeastern Calif. Chapter
2424 Arden Way, #450
Sacramento, CA 95825
(916) 921-5533

Northern Calif. Chapter
203 Willow St., #201
San Francisco, CA 94109
(415) 673-6882

San Diego Chapter
7675 Dagget Street, #330
San Diego, CA 92111
(619) 492-1094

Southern Calif. Chapter
4311 Wilshire Blvd., #530
Los Angeles, CA 90010
(213) 938-6111

Rocky Mountain Chapter
2280 South Albion St.
Denver, CO 80222
(303) 756-8622

Connecticut Chapter
1092 Elm Street
Rocky Hill, CT 06067
(203) 563-1177

Delaware Chapter
222 Philadelphia Pk., #1
Wilmington, DE 19809
(302) 764-8254

Metro Washington Chapter
1901 Ft. Myer Dr., #500
Arlington, VA 22209
(703) 276-7555

Florida Chapter
5211 Manatee Ave, W
Bradenton, FL 34209
(813) 795-3010

Georgia Chapter
2045 Peachtree Rd., #800
Atlanta, GA 30309
(404) 351-0454

Hawaii Chapter
Penthouse
Honfed Bank Building
45-1144 Kam Hwy
Kaneohe, HI 96744
(808) 235-3636

Idaho Chapter
4696 Overland Rd., #538
Boise, ID 83705
(208) 344-7102

Central Illinois Chapter
2621 N. Knoxville
Peoria, IL 61604
(309) 682-6600

Illinois Chapter
79 W Monroe St., #510
Chicago, IL 60603
(312) 782-1367

Indiana Chapter
8646 Guion Road
Indianapolis, IN 46268
(317) 879-0321

Iowa Chapter
8410 Hickman, Suite A
Des Moines, IA 50325
(515) 278-0636

Kansas Chapter
1602 East Waterman
Wichita, KS 67211
(316) 263-0116

Kentucky Chapter
3900 B. DuPont Sq. S
Louisville, KY 40207
(502) 893-9771

Louisiana Chapter
3955 Government St., #7
Baton Rouge, LA 70806
(504) 387-6932

Maine Chapter
37 Mill Street
Brunswick, ME 04011
(207) 729-4453

Maryland Chapter
3 Lan Lea Drive
Lutherville, MD 21093
(301) 561-8090

Massachusetts Chapter
450 Chatham Center
29 Crafts Street
Newton, MA 02160
(617) 244-1800

Michigan Chapter
23999 NW Hwy., #210
Southfield, MI 48075
(313) 350-3030

Minnesota Chapter
122 W. Franklin, #215
Minneapolis, MN 55404
(612) 874-1201

Mississippi Chapter
6055 Ridgewood Road
Jackson, MS 39211
(601) 956-3371

Eastern Missouri Chapter
7315 Manchester
St. Louis, MO 63143
(314) 644-3488

Western Missouri Chapter
8301 State Line, #200
Kansas City, MO 64114
(816) 361-7002

Montana Chapter
1239 North 28th
Billings, MT 59101
(406) 248-7602

Nebraska Chapter
2229 N 91st Court, #33
Omaha, NE 68134
(402) 391-8000

Nevada Chapter
3850 W Desert Inn, #108
Las Vegas, NV 89102
(702) 367-1626

New Hampshire Chapter
P.O. Box 369
35 Pleasant Street
Concord, NH 03302
(603) 224-9322

New Jersey Chapter
200 Middlesex Turnpike
Iselin, NJ 08830
(201) 283-4300

New Mexico Chapter
124 Alvarado, SE
Post Office Box 8022
Albuquerque, NM 87108
(505) 265-1545

Central New York Chapter
Pickard Building, #123
5858 East Molloy Road
Syracuse, NY 13211
(315) 455-8553

Genessee Valley Chapter
One Mount Hope Rd.
Rochester, NY 14620
(716) 423-9490

Long Island Chapter
501 Walt Whitman Rd.
Melville, NY 11747
(516) 427-8272

New York Chapter
67 Irving Place
New York, NY 10003
(212) 477-8310

Northeastern N.Y. Chapter
1237 Central Avenue
Albany, NY 12205
(518) 459-5082

Western N.Y. Chapter
1370 Niagara Falls Blvd.
Tonawanda, NY 14150
(716) 837-8600

North Carolina Chapter
3801 Wake Forest Rd., #115
Durham, NC 27703
(919) 596-3360

Dakota Chapter
115 Roberts Street
Fargo, ND 58102
(701) 237-3310

Central Ohio Chapter
2501 North Star Road
Columbus, OH 43221
(614) 488-0777

NE Ohio Chapter
23811 Chagrin Blvd.
Chagrin Plaza E, #210
Beachwood, OH 44122
(216) 831-7000

NW Ohio Chapter
2650 North Reynolds Rd.
Toledo, OH 43615
(419) 537-0888

SW Ohio Chapter
7811 Laurel Avenue
Cincinnati, OH 45243
(513) 271-4545

Eastern Oklahoma Chapter
4520 W Harvard, #100
Tulsa, OK 74135
(918) 743-4526

Oklahoma Chapter
   2915 Classen Blvd., #325
   Oklahoma City, OK 73106
   (405) 521-0066

Oregon Chapter
   4445 SW Barbur Blvd.
   Portland, OR 97201
   (503) 222-7246

Central Pennsyl. Chapter
   P.O. Box 668
   2019 Chestnut Street
   Camp Hill, PA 17011
   (717) 763-0900

Eastern Pennsyl. Chapter
   1217 Sansom Street
   Philadelphia, PA 19107
   (215) 574-9480

Western Pennsyl. Chapter
   Warner Centre—Fl. 5
   332 Fifth Avenue
   Pittsburgh, PA 15222
   (412) 566-1645

Rhode Island Chapter
   850 Waterman Avenue
   East Providence, RI 02914
   (401) 434-5792

South Carolina Chapter
   P.O. Box 11967
   Columbia, SC 29202
   (803) 254-6702

Middle-East Tenn. Chapter
   210 25th Ave. N, #523
   Nashville, TN 37203
   (615) 329-3431

West Tennessee Chapter
   6084 Apple Tree Dr., #4
   Memphis, TN 38115
   (901) 365-7080

North Texas Chapter
   2824 Swiss Avenue
   Dallas, TX 75204
   (214) 826-4361

Northwest Texas Chapter
   3145 McCart Avenue
   Fort Worth, TX 76110
   (817) 926-7733

South Central Tex. Chapter
   1407 N Main
   San Antonio, TX 78212
   (512) 224-8222

Texas Gulf Coast Chapter
   7660 Wood Way, #540
   Houston, TX 77063
   (713) 785-2360

Utah Chapter
   1733 South 1100 East
   Salt Lake City, UT 84105
   (801) 486-4993

Vermont Chapter
   2 Church Street
   Richardson Pl. 3F
   Burlington, VT 05401
   (802) 864-4988

Virginia Chapter
   565 Southlake Blvd.
   Richmond, VA 23236
   (804) 379-7464

Washington State Chapter
   100 South King, #300
   Seattle, WA 98104
   (206) 622-1378

West Virginia Chapter
   PO Box 296
   Dunbar, WV 25064
   (304) 768-3667

Wisconsin Chapter
   8556 West National Ave.
   West Allis, WI 53227
   (414) 321-3933

Books

Arthritis: A Comprehensive Guide (3d ed.), Dr. James F. Fries, Addison-Wesley, Massachusetts, 1990.

The Arthritis Exercise Book, Semyon Krewer, Cornerstone Library/ Simon and Schuster, New York, 1981.

The Arthritis Helpbook (3d ed.), Dr. James F. Fries and Kate Lorig, Addison-Wesley, Massachusetts, 1990.

Arthritis: What Works, Dava Sobel and Arthur C. Klein, St. Martin's Press, New York, 1989.

Magazines

Arthritis Today (bimonthly)
Arthritis Foundation
1314 Spring St. NW
Atlanta, GA 30309.

INDEX

180

183